莎士比亚 经典戏剧系列

雅典的泰门

〔英〕莎士比亚 ○著
朱生豪 ○译

汉英对照

石油工业出版社

图书在版编目（CIP）数据

雅典的泰门：汉英对照 /（英）莎士比亚著；朱生豪译. —北京：石油工业出版社，2022.3
（莎士比亚经典戏剧系列）
ISBN 978-7-5183-4550-2

Ⅰ.①雅... Ⅱ.①莎... ②朱... Ⅲ.①英语—汉语—对照读物②悲剧—剧本—英国—中世纪 Ⅳ.
①H319.4：I

中国版本图书馆CIP数据核字（2021）第035113号

莎士比亚经典戏剧系列：雅典的泰门（汉英对照）
〔英〕莎士比亚　著　朱生豪　译

出版发行：石油工业出版社
　　　　　（北京市朝阳区安华里二区1号楼　100011）
网　　　址：www.petropub.com
编　辑　部：（010）64523684
图书营销中心：（010）64523633
经　　　销：全国新华书店
印　　　刷：金世嘉元（唐山）印务有限公司

2022年3月第1版　2022年3月第1次印刷
880毫米×1230毫米　开本：1/32　印张：6.5
字数：200千字

定价：36.00元
（如发现印装质量问题，我社图书营销中心负责调换）
版权所有，侵权必究

前　言

　　莎士比亚，一个辉映世界文学史的名字；莎士比亚戏剧，世界文学史上永恒的经典，引无数后来者阅读、膜拜。为了满足广大读者对莎士比亚作品孜孜不倦的追求，我们推出了这套"莎士比亚经典戏剧系列"丛书，精选十二部具有代表性的作品，包括四大悲剧、四大喜剧，以及其他四部不容错过的经典戏剧作品，以中英文对照的方式，呈现给读者朋友们。

　　英国前首相丘吉尔曾说："我宁愿失去一个印度，也不愿失去一个莎士比亚。"莎士比亚（1564—1616），英国文艺复兴时期伟大的剧作家，一生写下了154首十四行诗、2首长诗以及38部戏剧，被誉为"人类文学奥林匹斯山上的宙斯"。

　　尽管莎士比亚逝世已有四百多年，他的作品至今依旧脍炙人口。正如当初与他同时代的英国诗人本·琼森所称赞："他不属于一个时代而属于所有的世纪。"但是，作为一个生活在21世纪的中国的普通人，我们为什么要读莎士比亚呢？

　　除了其戏剧荡气回肠的语言、穿透人性的哲理，莎士比亚已经成为一个文化符号，其作品已成为与古希腊神话、《圣经》并列的西方文化母体之一。了解莎士比亚戏剧，是我们理解西方文化的一个重要途径。

　　即使没有读过莎士比亚的作品，我们也都听说过这句话：一千个读者，就有一千个哈姆莱特。莎士比亚作品中最具代表性的便是四大悲剧——《哈姆莱特》《奥赛罗》《李尔王》《麦克白》。《哈姆莱特》是对人的原罪的追溯，《奥赛罗》让我们明白人心实在是经不起试探，《李尔王》揭示了伦理道德的困惑，《麦克白》使我们见识了命运对人类的玩弄。这四大悲剧，描写的无论是怒火如仇的复仇、穷凶极恶的罪行，还是缠绵悱恻的爱情、野心勃勃的宫斗，都极富哲理，句句锥心，让人难以释怀。

喜剧在莎士比亚戏剧创作中也占有相当分量，莎士比亚四大喜剧包括《仲夏夜之梦》《威尼斯商人》《第十二夜》《皆大欢喜》，这些作品以机智风趣的语言将浪漫、抒情、讽刺的风格发挥得淋漓尽致，戏谑当中渗透着些许悲剧意味，更显其喜，蕴含着人文主义者的美好理想，以及对人类光明前途的展望。《仲夏夜之梦》讲述的是有情人终成眷属的故事，《威尼斯商人》成功地塑造了唯利是图的四大吝啬鬼形象之一——夏洛克，《第十二夜》赞美了爱情自由和个性解放，《皆大欢喜》反映了莎士比亚理想中的以善胜恶的美好境界。

除了四大悲剧与四大喜剧，莎士比亚的经典剧目还有《罗密欧与朱丽叶》《温莎的风流娘儿们》《雅典的泰门》《无事生非》。《罗密欧与朱丽叶》讲述了意大利贵族凯普莱特女儿朱丽叶与蒙太古的儿子罗密欧诚挚相爱，誓言相依，但因两家世代为仇而受到阻挠的故事，《温莎的风流娘儿们》是唯一一部以英国现实为背景反映市民生活的剧本，《雅典的泰门》揭露了拜金主义的罪恶，《无事生非》围绕爱情主题并行两条线索，诠释了美好的爱情。

俄国评论家别林斯基说："他（莎士比亚）的每一个剧本都是一个世界的缩影，包含着整个现在、过去及未来。"时至今日，我们仍然能在这四百年前的戏剧中，看到自己的影子。如果你有书架，你一定要摆放一套莎士比亚,因为你几乎所有的人生困惑,莎士比亚都有解药。读莎士比亚,提高的不仅是你的文学素养,还有你的主观幸福感。

好的作品还要有好的翻译。朱生豪(1912—1944),浙江嘉兴人,从24岁起开始翻译莎士比亚作品,直至32岁病逝。他所翻译的莎剧,是公认最能显现莎剧神韵、最通俗易懂的译本,正如他自己所说:"余译此书之宗旨,第一在求于尽可能之范围内,保持原作之神韵;必不得已而求其次,亦必以明白晓畅之字句,忠实传达原文之意趣;而于逐字逐句对照式之硬译,则未敢赞同。"这套莎士比亚经典戏剧系列,即选用了朱生豪先生的译本,希望给您带来一场不同凡响的阅读旅程。

《雅典的泰门》导读

《雅典的泰门》是莎士比亚创作的最后一部悲剧，创作于1607—1608年。莎士比亚的戏剧，大多展示了家庭伦理和两性关系，比如父母子女关系、兄弟姐妹关系、情侣关系和夫妻关系，然而《雅典的泰门》却是游离于该法则之外的特例。剧中所有人物彼此之间没有血缘关系，主人公泰门更是没有家庭，也没有伴侣。

雅典富有的贵族泰门，因为热情诚恳，乐善好施，其周围很快聚集了一群阿谀奉承的"朋友"，其中有市井小民，也有达官显贵。他们假借追随他之名，伺机骗取他的钱财。泰门轻信其酒肉朋友的甜言蜜语，对哲学家艾帕曼特斯的提醒不以为然，对仆人的忠告也充耳不闻。奢华的宴会、慷慨的赠予很快耗尽了他的家产，他负债累累，失去了往日的气派和尊严。但是，泰门认为贫困也许是一种幸运，他相信贫穷不可怕，毕竟他有这么多朋友。然而，现实是如此残酷，昔日朋友翻脸无情，对他反唇相讥，甚至恩将仇报、乘人之危、落井下石。债主们找上门来，无情地逼他还债，几乎将泰门逼上绝境。这些人完全不感念于昔日在泰门宴请时大吃大喝的情景以及在泰门门下得到的丰厚赏赐。面对残酷的现实，泰门终于醒悟过来，明白了他们从来也没爱过他，他们爱的只是他的金钱。

于是，他决定再举行一次宴会，邀请过去的常客和社会名流。这些人误以为泰门原来是装穷来考验他们的忠诚，蜂拥而至，虚情假意地向泰门嘘寒问暖。泰门揭开盖子，把盘子里的热水泼在客人的脸上和身上，把他们痛骂了一顿。从此，泰门离开了这座城市，躲进荒凉的洞穴,以树根充饥,过着野兽般的生活。有一天他在挖树根时发现了一堆金子,他回忆起了金钱带来的不幸,决定用金钱来惩罚罪恶的人类:支持被驱逐的将军艾西巴第斯攻打雅典,鼓励盗贼偷窃和凶杀,让贪恋钱财的妓女传播疾病。他恶毒地诅咒人类和黄金,最后在绝望中孤独地死去。泰门最后葬身在人迹罕至的海边,墓碑上刻着:"我,泰门,安息于此;我在世时恨一切人。"

歌德说:"莎士比亚与世界精神结伴,他也像世界精神一样看透了这个世界,什么都不能瞒过他。"这部戏剧中泰门关于金子的经典独白:"金子!黄黄的,光闪闪的,只要有这一点点,就可以使黑的变成白的,丑的变成美的,错的变成对的,卑贱者变成尊贵者,老人变成少年,懦夫变成勇士。这黄色的奴隶——可以使异族同盟,同宗分裂;它可以使鸡皮黄脸的寡妇重做新娘,即使她的尊容可以使身染恶疮的人见了呕吐,有了这东西——也会恢复三春的娇艳;它会使冰炭化为胶漆,仇敌互相亲吻,它会说任何方言,使每一个人唯命是从;它是一尊了不起的神明,即使它住在比猪巢还卑劣的庙宇里,也会使人顶礼膜拜。" 这段话反映了在一个唯利是图的社会里,友谊是没有立足之地的。

该戏剧反映了人文主义理想的破灭,深刻揭露了当时金钱主宰一切的残酷现实和拜金主义的种种罪恶。卡尔·马克思曾指出:"在《雅典的泰门》中,莎士比亚揭示了金钱的两个本质。金钱是可见之神,可使人性逆转、天性悖然,可使天下大乱、万物违和、兄弟阋墙;金钱是人尽可夫的娼妓,也是使全天下勾搭成奸的掮客,简言之,我们崇拜金钱,金钱却扭曲我们的价值观,把世间一切关系转换成了商业交易。"

译者自序

于世界文学史中，足以笼罩一世，凌越千古，卓然为词坛之宗匠，诗人之冠冕者，其唯希腊之荷马，意大利之但丁，英之莎士比亚，德之歌德乎。此四子者，各于其不同之时代及环境中，发为不朽之歌声。然荷马史诗中之英雄，既与吾人之现实生活相去过远，但丁之天堂地狱，复与近代思想诸多抵牾；歌德去吾人较近，彼实为近代精神之卓越的代表。然以超脱时空限制一点而论，则莎士比亚之成就，实远在三子之上。盖莎翁笔下之人物，虽多为古代之贵族阶级，然其所发掘者，实为古今中外贵贱贫富人人所同具之人性。故虽经三百余年以后，不仅其书为全世界文学之士所耽读，其剧本且在各国舞台与银幕上历久搬演而弗衰，盖由其作品中具有永久性与普遍性，故能深入人心如此耳。

中国读者耳莎翁大名已久，文坛知名之士，亦尝将其作品译出多种，然历观坊间各译本失之于粗疏草率者尚少，失之于拘泥生硬者实繁有徒。拘泥字句之结果，不仅原作神味，荡焉无存，甚至艰深晦涩，有若天书，令人不能卒读，此则译者之过，莎翁不能任其咎者也。

余笃嗜莎剧，尝首尾严诵全集至十余遍，于原作精神，自觉颇有会心。廿四年春，得前辈同事詹文浒先生之鼓励，始着手为翻译全集之尝试。越年战事发生，历年来辛苦搜集之各种莎集版本，及诸家注释考证批评之书，不下一二百册，悉数毁于炮火，仓卒中唯携出牛津版全集一册，及译稿数本而已。厥后转辗流徙，为生活而奔波，更无暇晷，以续未竟之志。及卅一年春，目睹事变日亟，闭户家居，摈绝外务，始得专心一志，致力译事。虽贫穷疾病，交相煎迫，而埋头伏案，握管不辍。凡前后历十年而全稿完成，夫以译莎工作之艰巨，十年之功，不可云久，然毕生精力，殆已尽注于兹矣。

余译此书之宗旨，第一在求最大可能之范围内，保持原作之神韵；必不得已而求其次，亦必以明白晓畅之字句，忠实传达原文之意趣；而于逐字逐句对照式之硬译，则未敢赞同。凡遇原文中与中国语法不合之处，往往再四咀嚼，不惜全部更易原文之结构，务使作者之命意豁然呈露，不为晦涩之字句所掩蔽。每译一段竟，必先自拟为读者，察阅译文中有无暧昧不明之处。又必自拟为舞台上之演员，审辨语调之是否顺口，音节之是否调和，一字一句之未惬，往往苦思累日。然才力所限，未能尽符理想；乡居僻陋，既无参考之书籍，又鲜质疑之师友。谬误之处，自知不免。所望海内学人，惠予纠正，幸甚幸甚！

生豪书于三十三年四月

Contents
目 录

DRAMATIS PERSONAE / 2
剧中人物 / 3

Act I / 6
第一幕 / 7

Act II / 50
第二幕 / 51

Act III / 72
第三幕 / 73

Act IV / 118
第四幕 / 119

Act V / 168
第五幕 / 169

DRAMATIS PERSONAE

TIMON a noble Athenian

LUCIUS

LUCULLUS } flattering lords

SEMPRONIUS

VENTIDIUS one of Timon's false friends

APEMANTUS a churlish philosopher

ALCIBIADES an Athenian captain

FLAVIUS steward to Timon

FLAMINIUS

LUCILIUS } Timon's servants

SERVILIUS

CAPHIS

PHILOTUS

TITUS } Servants to usurers

LUCIUS' SERVANT

HORTENSIUS

Servants of VARRO and ISIDORE

Three STRANGERS

剧中人物

泰　　门　雅典贵族
路　歇　斯 ⎫
路 库 勒 斯 ⎬ 谄媚的贵族
辛 普 洛 涅 斯 ⎭
文 提 狄 斯　泰门的负心友人之一
艾 帕 曼 特 斯　性情乖僻的哲学家
艾 西 巴 第 斯　雅典将官
弗 莱 维 斯　泰门的管家
弗 莱 米 涅 斯 ⎫
路 西 律 斯 ⎬ 泰门的仆人
塞 维 律 斯 ⎭
凯　菲　斯 ⎫
菲 洛 特 斯 ⎪
泰　特　斯 ⎬ 泰门债主的仆人
路 歇 斯 之 仆 ⎪
霍 坦 歇 斯 ⎭
凡罗及艾西铎的仆人
三路人

AN OLD ATHENIAN

A PAGE

A FOOL

A POET

A PAINTER

A JEWELLER

A MERCHANT *who trades in silks*

PHRYNIA ⎫
           ⎬ *whores with Alcibiades*
TIMANDRA ⎭

Other LORDS, SENATORS, Servants, BANDITTI, and Attendants.

CUPID and MASQVERS

SCENE

Athens and the neighbouring woods

雅典老人

侍童

弄人

诗人、画师、宝石匠及商人

菲莉妮娅 ⎱
提曼德拉 ⎰ 艾西巴第斯的情妇

贵族、元老、将士、兵士、窃贼、侍从等

化装跳舞中扮丘比特及阿玛宗女战士者

地　点

雅典及附近森林

Act I

SCENE I Athens. A Hall in Timon's House.

[*Enter Poet, Painter, Jeweller, Merchant (a Mercer) at several doors.*]

POET	Good day, sir.
PAINTER	I am glad you're well.
POET	I have not seen you long. How goes the world?
PAINTER	It wears, sir, as it grows.
POET	Ay, that's well known.
	But what particular rarity? What strange,
	Which manifold record not matches? See,
	Magic of bounty, all these spirits thy power
	Hath conjured to attend. I know the merchant.
PAINTER	I know them both: th'other's a jeweller.
MERCHANT	[*To Jeweller.*] O, 'tis a worthy lord.
JEWELLER	Nay, that's most fixed.
MERCHANT	A most incomparable man, breathed, as it were,
	To an untirable and continuate goodness:
	He passes.
JEWELLER	I have a jewel here —
MERCHANT	O, pray let's see't. For the lord Timon, sir?
JEWELLER	If he will touch the estimate. But for that —
POET	'When we for recompense have praised the vile.
	It stains the glory in that happy verse
	Which aptly sings the good.'

第 一 幕

第一场 雅典。泰门家中的厅堂

（诗人、画师、宝石匠、商人及余人等自各门分别上）

诗 人		早安，先生。
画 师		您好！
诗 人		好久不见了。近况怎样啊？
画 师		先生，变得一天不如一天了。
诗 人		嗯，那是谁都知道的，可是有什么特别新鲜的事情，有什么奇闻怪事，为我们浩如烟海的载籍中所未之前睹的？瞧，慷慨的魔力！群灵都被你召唤前来，听候驱使了。我认识这个商人。
画 师		这两个人我都认识；有一个是宝石匠。
商 人		（对宝石匠）啊！真是一位贤德的贵人。
宝石匠		嗯，那是谁都不能否认的。
商 人		一位举世无比的人，他的生活的目的，好像就是永不厌倦，继续不断地行善。像他这样的人，真是难得！
宝石匠		我带着一颗宝石在这儿——
商 人		啊！倒要见识见识。先生，这是送给泰门大爷的吗？
宝石匠		要是他能出一个价格；可是——
诗 人		诗句当为美善而歌颂， 倘因贪利而赞美丑恶， 就会降低风雅的身价。

MERCHANT	[*Looks at the jewel.*] 'Tis a good form.
JEWELLER	And rich: here is a water, look ye.
PAINTER	[*To Poet.*] You are rapt, sir, in some work, some dedication
	To the great lord.
POET	A thing slipped idly from me.
	Our poesy is as a gum, which oozes
	From whence 'tis nourished.The fire i'th' flint
	Shows not till it be struck: our gentle flame
	Provokes itself and like the current flies
	Each bound it chafes. What have you there?
PAINTER	A picture, sir. When comes your book forth?
POET	Upon the heels of my presentment, sir.
	Let's see your piece.
PAINTER	[*Shows the painting.*] 'Tis a good piece.
POET	So 'tis: this comes off well and excellent.
PAINTER	Indifferent.
POET	Admirable. How this grace
	Speaks his own standing! What a mental power
	This eye shoots forth! How big imagination
	Moves in this lip! To th'dumbness of the gesture
	One might interpret.
PAINTER	It is a pretty mocking of the life.
	Here is a touch: is't good?
POET	I will say of it,
	It tutors nature: artificial strife
	Lives in these touches livelier than life.
	[*Enter certain Senators. They pass over the stage.*]
PAINTER	How this lord is followed!

商 人		（观宝石）这宝石的式样很不错。
宝石匠		它的色彩也很美丽，您瞧那光泽多好。
画 师		（对诗人）先生，您又在吟哦您的大作了吗？一定又是献给这位贵人的什么诗篇了。
诗 人		偶然想起来的几个句子。我们的诗歌就像树脂一样，会从它滋生的地方分泌出来。燧石中的火不打是不会出来的，我们的灵感的火焰却会自然激发，像流水般冲击着岸边。您手里是什么东西？
画 师		一幅图画，先生。您的大著几时出版？
诗 人		等我把它呈献给这位贵人以后，就可以和世人相见了。可不可以让我欣赏欣赏您的妙绘？
画 师		（展示画作）见笑得很。
诗 人		画得很好，真是神来之笔。
画 师		谬奖谬奖。
诗 人		佩服佩服！瞧这姿态多么优美！这一双眼睛里闪耀着多少智慧！这一双嘴唇上流露着多少丰富的想象！在这默然无语的神情中间，蕴蓄着无限的深意。
画 师		这是一幅惟妙惟肖的画像。这一笔很传神，您看怎样？
诗 人		简直是巧夺天工，就是真的人也不及老兄笔下这样生趣盎然。

（若干元老上，他们自舞台前经过）

画 师		这位贵人真是前呼后拥！

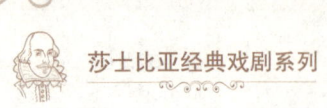
莎士比亚经典戏剧系列

POET	The senators of Athens, happy men.
PAINTER	Look, more.
POET	[*Shows the poem.*] You see this confluence, this great flood of visitors.
	I have in this rough work shaped out a man
	Whom this beneath world doth embrace and hug
	With amplest entertainment: my free drift
	Halts not particularly, but moves itself
	In a wide sea of wa — no levelled malice
	Infects one comma in the course I hold —
	But flies an eagle flight, bold and forth on,
	Leaving no tract behind.
PAINTER	How shall I understand you?
POET	I will unbolt to you.
	You see how all conditions, how all minds,
	As well of glib and slipp'ry creatures as
	Of grave and austere quality, tender down
	Their services to Lord Timon: his large fortune
	Upon his good and gracious nature hanging
	Subdues and properties to his love and tendance
	All sorts of hearts; yea, from the glass-faced flatterer
	To Apemantus, that few things loves better
	Than to abhor himself — even he drops down
	The knee before him, and returns in peace
	Most rich in Timon's nod.
PAINTER	I saw them speak together.
POET	Sir, I have upon a high and pleasant hill
	Feigned Fortune to be throned: the base o'th' mount
	Is ranked with all deserts, all kind of natures

诗　　人　都是雅典的元老；幸福的人！

画　　师　瞧，还有！

诗　　人　（展示诗篇）您瞧这一大群蝇营蚁附的宾客。在我的拙作中间，我勾画出了一个受尽世俗爱宠的人；可是我并不单单着力作个人的描写，我让我的恣肆的笔锋在无数的模型之间活动，不带一丝恶意，只是像凌空的鹰隼一样，一往直前，不留下一丝痕迹。

画　　师　您的意思我有点儿不大懂得。

诗　　人　我可以解释给您听。您瞧各种不同地位不同性情的人，无论是轻浮油滑的，或是严肃庄重的，都愿意为泰门大爷效劳服役；他的巨大的财产，再加上他的善良和蔼的天性，征服了各种不同的人，使他们乐于向他输诚致敬；从那些脸上反映出主人的喜怒的谄媚者起，直到憎恨自己的艾帕曼特斯，一个个在他的面前屈膝，只要泰门点点头，就可以使他们满载而归。

画　　师　我曾经看见他跟艾帕曼特斯在一起谈话。

诗　　人　先生，我假定命运的女神端坐在一座巍峨而幽美的山

                    That labour on the bosom of this sphere
                    To propagate their states, amongst them all
                    Whose eyes are on this sovereign lady fixed
                    One do I personate of Lord Timon's frame,
                    Whom Fortune with her ivory hand wafts to her,
                    Whose present grace to present slaves and servants
                    Translates his rivals.

PAINTER   'Tis conceived to scope.
                    This throne, this Fortune, and this hill, methinks,
                    With one man beckoned from the rest below,
                    Bowing his head against the steepy mount
                    To climb his happiness, would be well expressed
                    In our condition.

POET   Nay, sir, but hear me on.
                    All those which were his fellows but of late,
                    Some better than his value, on the moment
                    Follow his strides, his lobbies fill with tendance,
                    Rain sacrificial whisperings in his ear,
                    Make sacred even his stirrup, and through him
                    Drink the free air.

PAINTER   Ay, marry, what of these?
POET   When Fortune in her shift and change of mood
                    Spurns down her late beloved, all his dependants,
                    Which laboured after him to the mountain's top
                    Even on their knees and hands, let him fly down,
                    Not one accompanying his declining foot.

PAINTER   'Tis common:
                    A thousand moral paintings I can show
                    That shall demonstrate these quick blows of Fortune's

上；在那山麓下面，有无数智愚贤不肖的人在那儿劳心劳力，追求世间的名利，他们的眼睛都一致注视着这位主宰一切的女神；我把其中一个人代表泰门，命运女神用她象牙一样洁白的手招引他到她的身边；他是她眼前的恩宠，他的敌人也一齐变成了他的奴仆。

画　　师　果然是很巧妙的设想。我想这一个宝座，这一位命运女神和这一座山，在这山下的许多人中间，只有一个人得到女神的招手，这个人正弓着身子向峻峭的山崖爬去，攀登到幸福的顶端，很可以表现出我们这儿的情形。

诗　　人　不，先生，听我说下去。那些在不久以前还是和他同样地位的人，也有一些本来胜过他的人，现在都跟在他后面亦步亦趋；他的接待室里挤满了关心他的起居的人，他的耳朵中充满了一片有如向神圣祷告那样的低语；连他的马镫也是神圣的，他们从他那里呼吸到自由的空气。

画　　师　好，那便怎么样呢？

诗　　人　当命运突然改变了心肠，把她的宠儿一脚踢下山坡的时候，那些攀龙附凤之徒，本来跟在他后面匍匐膝行的，这时候便会冷眼看他跌落，没有一个人做他患难中的同伴。

画　　师　那是人类的通性。我可以画出一千幅醒世的图画，比

                More pregnantly than words. Yet you do well
To show Lord Timon that mean eyes have seen
The foot above the head.
[*Trumpets sound. Enter Lord Timon with Lucilius and other servants following, addressing himself courteously to every suitor and then speaking with a Messenger.*]

TIMON   Imprisoned is he, say you?
MESSENGER   Ay, my good lord: five talents is his debt,
His means most short, his creditors most strait.
Your honourable letter he desires
To those have shut him up, which failing,
Periods his comfort.
TIMON   Noble Ventidius! Well,
I am not of that feather to shake off
My friend when he must need me. I do know him
A gentleman that well deserves a help,
Which he shall have: I'll pay the debt and free him.
MESSENGER   Your lordship ever binds him.
TIMON   Commend me to him. I will send his ransom,
And being enfranchised, bid him come to me:
'Tis not enough to help the feeble up,
But to support him after. Fare you well.
MESSENGER   All happiness to your honour. [*Exit.*]
[*Enter an old Athenian.*]
OLD MAN   Lord Timon, hear me speak.
TIMON   Freely, good father.
OLD MAN   Thou hast a servant named Lucilius.
TIMON   I have so: what of him?

语言更有力地说明祸福无常的真理。但是你也不妨用文字向泰门大爷陈述一个道理，指出眼光浅近的人往往会把黑白混淆起来。

（喇叭声。泰门上，向每一请求者殷勤周旋；一使者奉文提狄斯差遣前来，趋前与泰门谈话；路西律斯及其他仆人随后）

泰 门 你说他下了监狱了吗？

使 者 是，大爷。他欠了五泰伦的债，他的手头非常困难，他的债主催逼得很厉害。他请您写一封信去给那些拘禁他的人，否则他什么安慰也没有了。

泰 门 尊贵的文提狄斯！好，我不是一个在朋友有困难时把他丢弃不顾的人。我知道他是一位值得帮助的绅士，我一定要帮助他。我愿意替他还债，使他恢复自由。

使 者 他永远不会忘记您的大恩。

泰 门 替我向他致意。我就会把他的赎金送去，他出狱以后，请他到我这儿来。单单把软弱无力的人扶了起来是不够的，必须有人随时搀扶他，照顾他。再见。

使 者 愿大爷有福！（下）

（一雅典老人上）

老 人 泰门大爷，听我说句话。

泰 门 你说吧，好老人家。

老 人 你有一个名叫路西律斯的仆人。

泰 门 是的，他怎么啦？

OLD MAN	Most noble Timon, call the man before thee.
TIMON	[*Calls.*] Attends he here or no? Lucilius!
LUCILIUS	[*Comes forward.*] Here, at your lordship's service.
OLD MAN	This fellow here, Lord Timon, this thy creature,
	By night frequents my house. I am a man
	That from my first have been inclined to thrift,
	And my estate deserves an heir more raised
	Than one which holds a trencher.
TIMON	Well, what further?
OLD MAN	One only daughter have I, no kin else
	On whom I may confer what I have got:
	The maid is fair, o'th' youngest for a bride,
	And I have bred her at my dearest cost
	In qualities of the best. This man of thine
	Attempts her love: I prithee, noble lord,
	Join with me to forbid him her resort,
	Myself have spoke in vain.
TIMON	The man is honest.
OLD MAN	Therefore he will be, Timon:
	His honesty rewards him in itself,
	It must not bear my daughter.
TIMON	Does she love him?
OLD MAN	She is young and apt:
	Our own precedent passions do instruct us
	What levity's in youth.
TIMON	[*To Lucilius.*] Love you the maid?
LUCILIUS	Ay, my good lord, and she accepts of it.
OLD MAN	If in her marriage my consent be missing,
	I call the gods to witness, I will choose

老　　　人　最尊贵的泰门，把那家伙叫来。

泰　　　门　（呼唤）他在不在这儿？路西律斯！

路西律斯　（上前）有，大爷有什么吩咐？

老　　　人　这个家伙，泰门大爷，你这位尊价，晚上常常到我家里来。我一生克勤克俭，挣下了这份家产，可不能让一个做奴才的承继了去。

泰　　　门　嗯，还有些什么话？

老　　　人　我只有一个独生的女儿，要是我死了，也没有别的亲人可以接受我的遗产。我这孩子长得很美，还没有到结婚的年纪，我费了不少的钱，让她受最好的教育。你这个仆人却想勾引她。好大爷，请你帮帮忙，不许他去看她；我自己对他说过好多次，总是没用。

泰　　　门　这个人倒还老实。

老　　　人　所以你应该叫他不要做不老实的事，泰门。一个人老老实实，总有好处；可不能让他老实得把我的女儿也拐了去。

泰　　　门　你的女儿爱他吗？

老　　　人　她年纪太轻，容易受人诱惑；就是我们自己在年轻的时候，也是一样多愁善感的。

泰　　　门　（向路西律斯）你爱这位姑娘吗？

路西律斯　是，我的好大爷，她也接受我的爱。

老　　　人　要是她没有得到我的允许和别人结婚，我请天神作证，

	Mine heir from forth the beggars of the world,
	And dispossess her all.
TIMON	How shall she be endowed
	If she be mated with an equal husband?
OLD MAN	Three talents on the present; in future, all.
TIMON	This gentleman of mine hath served me long:
	To build his fortune I will strain a little,
	For 'tis a bond in men. Give him thy daughter:
	What you bestow, in him I'll counterpoise,
	And make him weigh with her.
OLD MAN	Most noble lord,
	Pawn me to this your honour, she is his.
TIMON	My hand to thee: mine honour on my promise.
LUCILIUS	Humbly I thank your lordship: never may
	That state or fortune fall into my keeping,
	Which is not owed to you!
	[*Exeunt Lucilius and Old Man.*]
POET	[*Presents the poem.*] Vouchsafe my labour, and long live your lordship!
TIMON	I thank you. You shall hear from me anon:
	Go not away. — [*To the Painter.*] What have you there, my friend?
PAINTER	[*Presents the painting.*] A piece of painting, which I do beseech
	Your lordship to accept.
TIMON	Painting is welcome.
	The painting is almost the natural man,
	For since dishonour traffics with man's nature,
	He is but outside: these pencilled figures are

　　　　　我要拣一个乞儿做我的后嗣,一个钱也不给她。

泰　　门　要是她嫁给一个门户相当的丈夫,你预备给她怎样一份嫁奁呢?

老　　人　先给她三泰伦;等我死了以后,我的全部财产都是她的。

泰　　门　这个人已经在我这儿做了很久的事;君子成人之美,我愿意破格帮助他这次。把你的女儿给他;你有多少陪嫁费,我也给他同样的数目,这样他就可以不致辱没令嫒了。

老　　人　最尊贵的大爷,您既然这么说,我一定遵命,她就是他的人了。

泰　　门　好,我们握手为定;我用我的名誉向你担保。

路西律斯　敬谢大爷,我的一切幸运,都是您所赐予的!(路西律斯及老人下)

诗　　人　(呈上诗稿)这一本拙作要请大爷指教。

泰　　门　谢谢您;您不久就可以得到我的答复;不要走开。(对画师)您有些什么东西,我的朋友?

画　　师　(呈上画作)是一幅画,请大爷收下了吧。

泰　　门　一幅画吗?很好很好。这幅画简直画得像活人一样;因为自从欺诈渗进了人们的天性中以后,人本来就只剩一个外表了。这些画像确实是一丝不苟。我很喜欢

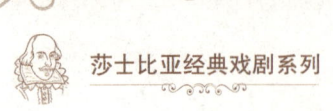

	Even such as they give out.I like your work,
	And you shall find I like it: wait attendance
	Till you hear further from me.
PAINTER	The gods preserve ye!
TIMON	Well fare you, gentleman: give me your hand,
	We must needs dine together. [*To the Jeweller.*]
	— Sir, your jewel
	Hath suffered under praise.
JEWELLER	What, my lord, dispraise?
TIMON	A mere satiety of commendations.
	If I should pay you for't as 'tis extolled
	It would unclew me quite.
JEWELLER	My lord, 'tis rated
	As those which sell would give: but you well know
	Things of like value differing in the owners,
	Are prized by their masters. Believe't, dear lord,
	You mend the jewel by the wearing it. [*Presents the jewel.*]
TIMON	Well mocked.
	[*Enter Apemantus.*]
MERCHANT	No, my good lord, he speaks the common tongue
	Which all men speak with him.
TIMON	Look, who comes here. Will you be chid?
JEWELLER	We'll bear with your lordship.
MERCHANT	He'll spare none.
TIMON	Good morrow to thee, gentle Apemantus!
APEMANTUS	Till I be gentle, stay thou for thy good morrow —
	When thou art Timon's dog, and these knaves honest.
TIMON	Why dost thou call them knaves? Thou know'st them not.

		您的作品,您就可以知道;请您等一等,我还有话对您说。
画	师	愿神明保佑您!
泰	门	回头见,先生;把您的手给我;您一定要陪我吃饭的。(对宝石匠)先生,您那颗宝石,我实在有点儿不敢领情。
宝石匠		怎么,大爷,宝石不好吗?
泰	门	简直是太好了。要是我按照人家对它所下的赞美那样的价值向您把它买了下来,恐怕我要倾家荡产了。
宝石匠		大爷,它的价格是按照市价估定的;可是您知道,同样价值的东西,往往因为主人的喜恶而分别高下。相信我,好大爷,要是您戴上了这宝石,它就会身价十倍了。(呈上珠宝)
泰	门	不要取笑。

(艾帕曼特斯上)

商	人	不,好大爷;他说的话不过是我们大家所要说的话。
泰	门	瞧,谁来啦?你们愿意挨一顿骂吗?
宝石匠		要是大爷不以为意,我们也愿意忍受他的侮辱。
商	人	他骂起人来是谁也不留情的。
泰	门	早安,善良的艾帕曼特斯!
艾帕曼特斯		等我善良以后,你再说你的早安吧;等你变成了泰门的狗,等这些恶人都变成好人以后,你再说你的早安吧。
泰	门	为什么你要叫他们恶人呢?你又不认识他们。

APEMANTUS	Are they not Athenians?
TIMON	Yes.
APEMANTUS	Then I repent not.
JEWELLER	You know me, Apemantus?
APEMANTUS	Thou know'st I do: I called thee by thy name.
TIMON	Thou art proud, Apemantus.
APEMANTUS	Of nothing so much as that I am not like Timon.
TIMON	Whither art going?
APEMANTUS	To knock out an honest Athenian's brains.
TIMON	That's a deed thou'lt die for.
APEMANTUS	Right, if doing nothing be death by th' law.
TIMON	How lik'st thou this picture, Apemantus?
APEMANTUS	The best, for the innocence.
TIMON	Wrought he not well that painted it?
APEMANTUS	He wrought better that made the painter, and yet he's but a filthy piece of work.
PAINTER	You're a dog.
APEMANTUS	Thy mother's of my generation: what's she, if I be a dog?
TIMON	Wilt dine with me, Apemantus?
APEMANTUS	No, I eat not lords.
TIMON	An thou shouldst, thou'dst anger ladies.
APEMANTUS	O, they eat lords: so they come by great bellies.
TIMON	That's a lascivious apprehension.
APEMANTUS	So thou apprehend'st it, take it for thy labour.
TIMON	How dost thou like this jewel, Apemantus?

艾帕曼特斯　他们不是雅典人吗？

泰　　　门　是的。

艾帕曼特斯　那么我没有叫错。

宝　石　匠　您认识我吗，艾帕曼特斯？

艾帕曼特斯　你知道我认识你；我刚才就叫过你的名字。

泰　　　门　你太骄傲了，艾帕曼特斯。

艾帕曼特斯　我感到最骄傲的是我不像泰门一样。

泰　　　门　你到哪儿去？

艾帕曼特斯　去砸碎一个正直的雅典人的脑袋。

泰　　　门　你干了那样的事，是要抵命的。

艾帕曼特斯　对了，要是干莫须有的事在法律上也要抵命的话。

泰　　　门　艾帕曼特斯，你喜欢这幅图画吗？

艾帕曼特斯　一幅好画，因为它并不伤人。

泰　　　门　画这幅画的人手法怎样？

艾帕曼特斯　造物创造出这个画师来，他的手法比这画师强多啦，虽然他创造出来的也不过是一件低劣的作品。

画　　　师　你是一条狗。

艾帕曼特斯　你的母亲是我的同类；倘然我是狗，她又是什么？

泰　　　门　你愿意陪我吃饭吗，艾帕曼特斯？

艾帕曼特斯　不，我是不吃那些贵人的。

泰　　　门　要是你吃了那些贵人，那些贵人的太太们要生气哩。

艾帕曼特斯　啊！她们自己才是吃贵人吃惯了的，所以吃得肚子那么大。

泰　　　门　你把事情看邪了。

艾帕曼特斯　那是你的看法，也难为你了。

泰　　　门　艾帕曼特斯，你喜欢这颗宝石吗？

APEMANTUS	Not so well as plain-dealing, which will not cost a man a dolt.
TIMON	What dost thou think 'tis worth?
APEMANTUS	Not worth my thinking. — How now, poet?
POET	How now, philosopher?
APEMANTUS	Thou liest.
POET	Art not one?
APEMANTUS	Yes.
POET	Then I lie not.
APEMANTUS	Art not a poet?
POET	Yes.
APEMANTUS	Then thou liest: look in thy last work, where thou hast feigned him a worthy fellow.
POET	That's not feigned, he is so.
APEMANTUS	Yes, he is worthy of thee, and to pay thee for thy labour. He that loves to be flattered is worthy o'th' flatterer. Heavens, that I were a lord!
TIMON	What wouldst do then, Apemantus?
APEMANTUS	E'en as Apemantus does now: hate a lord with my heart.
TIMON	What, thyself?
APEMANTUS	Ay.
TIMON	Wherefore?
APEMANTUS	That I had no angry wit to be a lord. — Art not thou a merchant?
MERCHANT	Ay, Apemantus.
APEMANTUS	Traffic confound thee, if the gods will not!
MERCHANT	If traffic do it, the gods do it.
APEMANTUS	Traffic's thy god, and thy god confound thee!

艾帕曼特斯　我喜欢真诚老实，它不花一文钱。

泰　　门　你想它值多少钱？

艾帕曼特斯　它不值得我去想它的价钱。你好，诗人！

诗　　人　你好，哲学家！

艾帕曼特斯　你说谎。

诗　　人　你不是哲学家吗？

艾帕曼特斯　是的。

诗　　人　那么我没有说谎。

艾帕曼特斯　你不是诗人吗？

诗　　人　是的。

艾帕曼特斯　那么你说谎；瞧你上一次的作品，你故意把他写成了一个好人。

诗　　人　那并不是假话；他的确是一个好人。

艾帕曼特斯　是的，他赏了你钱，所以他是一个好人：有了拍马的人，自然就有爱拍马的人。天哪，要是我也是一个贵人！

泰　　门　你做了贵人便怎么样呢，艾帕曼特斯？

艾帕曼特斯　我要是做了贵人，我就要像现在的艾帕曼特斯一样，从心底里痛恨一个贵人。

泰　　门　什么，痛恨你自己吗？

艾帕曼特斯　是的。

泰　　门　为什么呢？

艾帕曼特斯　恨我缺乏做老爷的熊脾气。——你是一个商人吗？

商　　人　是的，艾帕曼特斯。

艾帕曼特斯　要是神明不给你灾祸，那么让你在买卖上大倒其霉吧！

商　　人　要是我买卖失利，那就是神明给我的灾祸。

艾帕曼特斯　买卖就是你的神明，愿你的神明给你灾祸！

[Trumpet sounds. Enter a Messenger.]

TIMON What trumpet's that?

MESSENGER 'Tis Alcibiades, and some twenty horse
All of companionship.

TIMON Pray entertain them, give them guide to us.
[Exeunt some Attendants.]
You must needs dine with me.— Go not you hence
Till I have thanked you. — when dinner's done,
Show me this piece. — I am joyful of your sights.
[To all. Enter Alcibiades, with the rest.]
Most welcome, sir!

APEMANTUS So, so, there!
Aches contract and starve your supple joints!
That there should be small love amongst these sweet knaves,
And all this courtesy! The strain of man's bred out
Into baboon and monkey.

ALCIBIADES *[To Timon.]* Sir, you have saved my longing, and I feed
Most hungerly on your sight.

TIMON Right welcome, sir!
Ere we depart, we'll share a bounteous time
In different pleasures. Pray you, let us in. *[Exeunt all except Apemantus.]*
[Enter two Lords.]

FIRST LORD What time o'day is't, Apemantus?

APEMANTUS Time to be honest.

FIRST LORD That time serves still.

APEMANTUS The most accursèd thou, that still omitt'st it.

（号声起。一仆人上）

泰　　门　怎么有号声？

仆　　人　那是艾西巴第斯带着二十多人骑在马上来了。

泰　　门　你们去招待招待；领他们进来。（若干侍从下）你们必须陪我吃饭。等我谢过了你们的厚意以后再去。承你们各位光降，我非常高兴。

（艾西巴第斯率队上）。

泰　　门　欢迎得很，将军！

艾帕曼特斯　好，好！愿意痛把你们柔软的骨节扭成一团！这些温文和气的恶人彼此不怀好意，面子上却做得这样彬彬有礼！人类全都变成猴子啦。

艾西巴第斯　（对泰门）我已经想了您好久，今天能够看见您，真是大慰平生的饥渴。

泰　　门　欢迎欢迎！这次我们一定要好好地欢叙一下再分手。请一进去吧。（除了艾帕曼特斯均下）

（二贵族上）

贵　族　甲　现在是什么时候了，艾帕曼特斯？

艾帕曼特斯　现在是应该做个老实人的时候了。

贵　族　甲　人是无论什么时候都应该老老实实的。

艾帕曼特斯　那你就更加该死，你无论什么时候都是不老实的。

SECOND LORD Thou art going to Lord Timon's feast?
APEMANTUS Ay, to see meat fill knaves and wine heat fools.
SECOND LORD Fare thee well, fare thee well.
APEMANTUS Thou art a fool to bid me farewell twice.
SECOND LORD Why, Apemantus?
APEMANTUS Shouldst have kept one to thyself, for I mean to give thee none.
FIRST LORD Hang thyself!
APEMANTUS No, I will do nothing at thy bidding: make thy requests to thy friend.
SECOND LORD Away, unpeaceable dog, or I'll spurn thee hence!
APEMANTUS I will fly, like a dog, the heels o'th' ass. [*Exit.*]
FIRST LORD He's opposite to humanity. Come, shall we in,
And taste Lord Timon's bounty? He outgoes
The very heart of kindness.
SECOND LORD He pours it out. Plutus, the god of gold,
Is but his steward: no meed, but he repays
Sevenfold above itself: no gift to him
But breeds the giver a return exceeding
All use of quittance.
FIRST LORD The noblest mind he carries
That ever governed man.
SECOND LORD Long may he live in fortunes! Shall we in?
I'll keep you company. [*Exeunt.*]

贵族乙　你去参加泰门大爷的宴会吗？

艾帕曼特斯　是的，我要去看肉塞在恶汉的嘴里，酒灌在傻子的肚里。

贵族乙　再见，再见。

艾帕曼特斯　你是个傻瓜，向我说两次"再见"。

贵族乙　为什么，艾帕曼特斯？

艾帕曼特斯　你应该把一句"再见"留给你自己，因为我是不想向你说"再见"的。

贵族甲　你去上吊吧！

艾帕曼特斯　不，我不愿听从你的号令。你还是向你的朋友请求吧。

贵族乙　滚开，专爱吵架的狗！我要把你踢走了。

艾帕曼特斯　我要像一条狗一样逃开驴子的蹄子。（下）

贵族甲　他是个不近人情的家伙。来，我们进去，领略领略泰门大爷的盛情吧。他的慷慨仁慈，真是世间少有的。

贵族乙　他的恩惠是随时随地向人倾注的；财神普路托斯不过是他的管家。谁替他做了一件事，他总是给他价值七倍的酬劳；谁送给他什么东西，他的答礼总是超过一般酬酢的极限。

贵族甲　他有一颗比任何人更高贵的心。

贵族乙　愿他富贵长寿！我们进去吧。

　　　　　敢不奉陪。（同下）

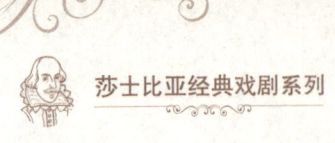

SCENE II   *The Same. A Room in Timon's House.*

[*Hautboys playing loud music. A great banquet served in: and then enter Lord Timon, the States, the Athenian, Lords, Alcibiades and, Ventidius, which Timon redeemed from prison. Then comes, dropping, after all,* Apemantus, *discontentedly, like himself.*]

VENTIDIUS Most honoured Timon,
It hath pleased the gods to remember my father's age,
And call him to long peace.
He is gone happy, and has left me rich:
Then, as in grateful virtue I am bound
To your free heart, I do return those talents,
Doubled with thanks and service, from whose help
I derived liberty. [*Offers money.*]

TIMON O, by no means,
Honest Ventidius. You mistake my love:
I gave it freely ever, and there's none
Can truly say he gives if he receives.
If our betters play at that game, we must not dare
To imitate them: faults that are rich are fair.

VENTIDIUS A noble spirit! [*The Lords stand ceremoniously.*]

TIMON Nay, my lords,
Ceremony was but devised at first
To set a gloss on faint deeds, hollow welcomes,
Recanting goodness, sorry ere 'tis shown,
But where there is true friendship, there needs none.
Pray, sit: more welcome are ye to my fortunes

第二场　同前。泰门家中的宴会厅

（高音笛奏闹乐。厅中设盛宴，弗莱维斯及其他仆人侍立；泰门、艾西巴第斯、众贵族元老、文提狄斯及侍从等上；艾帕曼特斯最后上，仍作倨傲不平之态）

文提狄斯　最可尊敬的泰门，神明因为眷念我父亲年老，召唤他去享受永久的安息；他已经安然去世，把他的财产遗留给我。这次多蒙您的大德鸿恩，使我脱离了缧绁之灾，现在我把那几个泰伦如数奉还，还要请您接受我的感恩图报的微忱。（递上钱款）

泰　　门　啊！这算什么，正直的文提狄斯？您误会我的诚意了；那笔钱是我送给您的，哪有给了人家再收回来之理？假如比我们高明的人这样做的话，我们也决不敢效法他们；有钱的人缺点也是优点。

文提狄斯　您的心肠太好了。（众垂手恭立，视泰门）

泰　　门　哎哟，各位大人，一切礼仪，都是为了文饰那些虚应故事的行为，言不由衷的欢迎，出尔反尔的殷勤而设

	Than my fortunes to me. [*They sit.*]
FIRST LORD	My lord, we always have confessed it.
APEMANTUS	Ho, ho, confessed it? Hanged it, have you not?
TIMON	O, Apemantus, you are welcome.
APEMANTUS	No, you shall not make me welcome:
	I come to have thee thrust me out of doors.
TIMON	Fie, thou'rt a churl: ye 've got a humour there
	Does not become a man: 'tis much to blame.
	They say, my lords, *Ira furor brevis est*,
	But yond man is ever angry.
	Go, let him have a table by himself,
	For he does neither affect company,
	Nor is he fit for't, indeed.
APEMANTUS	Let me stay at thine apperil, Timon:
	I come to observe; I give thee warning on't.
TIMON	I take no heed of thee; thou'rt an Athenian, therefore welcome. I myself would have no power: prithee let my meat make thee silent.
APEMANTUS	I scorn thy meat: 'twould choke me, for I should ne'er flatter thee. O you gods, what a number of men eats Timon, and he sees 'em not! It grieves me to see so many dip their meat in one man's blood, and all the madness is, he cheers them up too.
	I wonder men dare trust themselves with men.
	Methinks they should invite them without knives:
	Good for their meat, and safer for their lives.
	There's much example for't: the fellow that sits next him, now parts bread with him, pledges the breath of him in a divided draught, is the readiest man to kill

立的；如果有真实的友谊，这些虚伪的形式就该一律摈弃。请坐吧；我的财产欢迎你们分享，甚于我欢迎我自己的财产。（众就座）

贵族甲　大人，我们也常常这么说。

艾帕曼特斯　呵，呵！也这么说；哼，你们也这么说吗？

泰　门　啊！艾帕曼特斯，欢迎。

艾帕曼特斯　不，我不要你欢迎，我要你把我撵出门外去。

泰　门　呸！你是个伧夫；你的脾气太乖僻啦。各位大人，人家说，暴怒不终朝；可是这个人老是在发怒。去，给他一个人摆一张桌子，因为他不喜欢跟别人在一起，也不配跟别人在一起。

艾帕曼特斯　泰门，要是你不把我撵走，那你可不要怪我得罪你的客人；我是来做一个旁观者的。

泰　门　我不管你说什么；你是一个雅典人，所以我欢迎你。我自己没有力量封住你的嘴，请你让我的肉食使你静默吧。

艾帕曼特斯　我不要吃你的肉食；它会噎住我的喉咙，因为我永远不会谄媚你。神啊！多少人在吃泰门，他却看不见他们。我看见这许多人把他们的肉放在一个人的血里蘸着吃，我就心里难过；可是发了疯的他，却还在那儿殷勤劝客。我不知道人们怎么敢相信他们的同类；我想他们请客的时候，应当不备刀子，既可以省些肉，又可以防止生命的危险。这样的例子是很多的；现在坐在他的近旁，跟他一同切着面包、喝着同心酒的那个人，也就是第一个动手杀他的人；这种事情早就有

him: 't'as been proved. If I were a huge man, I should fear to drink at meals, Lest they should spy my windpipe's dangerous notes:

Great men should drink with harness on their throats.

TIMON My lord, in heart, and let the health go round.
SECOND LORD Let it flow this way, my good lord.
APEMANTUS 'Flow this way'? A brave fellow: he keeps his tides well. Those healths will make thee and thy state look ill, Timon.

Here's that which is too weak to be a sinner —

Honest water — which ne'er left man i'th' mire.

This and my food are equals, there's no odds.

Feasts are too proud to give thanks to the gods.

[*Apemantu's grace.*]

    Immortal gods, I crave no pelf.

    I pray for no man but myself:

    Grant I may never prove so fond,

    To trust man on his oath or bond,

    Or a harlot for her weeping

    Or a dog that seems a-sleeping,

    Or a keeper with my freedom,

    Or my friends if I should need 'em.

    Amen. So fall to't.

    Rich men sin, and I eat root.

Much good dich thy good heart, Apemantus! [*Eats.*]

TIMON Captain Alcibiades, your heart's in the field now.
ALCIBIADES My heart is ever at your service, my lord.
TIMON You had rather be at a breakfast of enemies than dinner of friends.

证明了。如果我是一个巨人，我一定不敢在进餐的时候喝酒；因为恐怕人家看准我的咽喉上的要害；大人物喝酒是应当用铁甲裹住咽喉的。

泰　　门　大人，今天一定要尽兴；大家干一杯，互祝健康吧。

贵 族 乙　好，大人，让酒像潮水一样流着吧。

艾帕曼特斯　像潮水一样流着！好家伙！他倒是惯会迎合潮流的。泰门泰门，这样一杯一杯地干下去，要把你的骨髓和你的家产都吸干了啊！我这儿只有一杯不会害人的淡酒，好水啊，你是不会叫人烂醉如泥的；这样的酒正好配着这样的菜。吃着大鱼大肉的人，是会高兴得忘记感谢神明的。（艾帕曼特斯做餐前祝谢词）

> 永生的神，我不要财宝，
> 我也不愿为别人祈祷：
> 保佑我不要做个呆子，
> 相信人们空口的盟誓；
> 也不要相信娼妓的泪；
> 也不要相信狗的假寐；
> 也不要相信我的狱吏，
> 或是我患难中的知己。
> 阿门！
> 好，吃吧；有钱的人犯了罪，我只好嚼嚼菜根。

（饮酒食肴）

泰　　门　艾西巴第斯将军，您的心现在一定在战场上驰骤吧。

艾西巴第斯　我的心是永远乐于供您驱使的，大人。

泰　　门　您一定欢喜和敌人们在一起早餐，甚于和朋友们在一起宴会。

莎士比亚经典戏剧系列

ALCIBIADES So they were bleeding new, my lord, there's no meat like 'em: I could wish my best friend at such a feast.

APEMANTUS Would all those flatterers were thine enemies then, that then thou mightst kill 'em and bid me to 'em!

FIRST LORD Might we but have that happiness, my lord, that you would once use our hearts whereby we might express some part of our zeals, we should think ourselves for ever perfect.

TIMON O, no doubt, my good friends, but the gods themselves have provided that I shall have much help from you: how had you been my friends else? Why have you that charitable title from thousands, did not you chiefly belong to my heart? I have told more of you to myself than you can with modesty speak in your own behalf, and thus far I confirm you. O you gods, think I, what need we have any friends if we should ne'er have need of 'em? They were the most needless creatures living, should we ne'er have use for 'em, and would most resemble sweet instruments hung up in cases that keeps their sounds to themselves. Why, I have often wished myself poorer, that I might come nearer to you. We are born to do benefits: and what better or properer can we call our own than the riches of our friends? O, what a precious comfort 'tis to have so many like brothers commanding one another's fortunes! O joy's e'en made away ere't can be born: mine eyes cannot hold out water, methinks. To forget their faults, I drink to you.

[*Weeps, and drinks.*]

APEMANTUS Thou weep'st to make them drink, Timon.

艾西巴第斯	大人，敌人的血是胜于一切美味的肉食的；我希望我的最好的朋友也能跟我在一起享受这样的盛宴。
艾帕曼特斯	但愿这些谄媚之徒全是你的敌人，那么你就可以把他们一起杀了，让我分享一杯羹。
贵　族　甲	大人，要是我们能够有那样的幸福，可以让我们的一片赤诚为您尽尺寸之劳，那么我们就可以自己觉得不虚此生了。
泰　　　门	啊！不要怀疑，我的好朋友们，天神早已注定我将要从你们得到许多的帮助了：否则你们怎么会做我的朋友呢？为什么在千万人中间，只有你们有那样一个名号：不是因为你们是我心上最亲近的人吗？你们因为谦逊而没有向我提起过的关于你们自己的话，我都向我自己说过了；这是我可以向你们证实的。我常常这么想着：神啊！要是我们永远没有需要我们的朋友的时候，那么我们何必要朋友呢？要是我们永远不需要他们的帮助，那么他们便是世上最无用的东西，就像深藏不用的乐器一样，没有人听得见它们美妙的声音。啊，我常常希望我自己再贫穷一些，那么我一定可以格外跟你们亲近一些。天生下我们来，就是要我们乐善好施；什么东西比我们朋友的财产更适宜于被我们称为我们自己的？啊！能够有这么许多人像自己的兄弟一样，彼此支配着各人的财产，这是一件多么可贵的乐事！我的眼睛里忍不住要流出眼泪来了；原谅我的软弱，我为各位干这一杯。（泣，干杯）
艾帕曼特斯	你简直是涕泣劝酒了，泰门。

SECOND LORD	[*To Timon.*] Joy had the like conception in our eyes And at that instant like a babe sprung up.
APEMANTUS	Ho, ho! I laugh to think that babe a bastard.
THIRD LORD	[*To Timon.*] I promise you, my lord, you moved me much.
APEMANTUS	Much!
	[*Sound tucket.*]
TIMON	What means that trump? How now?
	[*Enter servant.*]
SERVANT	Please you, my lord, there are certain ladies most desirous of admittance.
TIMON	Ladies? What are their wills?
SERVANT	There comes with them a forerunner, my lord, which bears that office to signify their pleasures.
TIMON	I pray, let them be admitted.
	[*Enter Cupid with the masque of Ladies. The Masquers stay back.*]
CUPID	Hail to thee, worthy Timon, and to all that Of his bounties taste! The five best senses Acknowledge thee their patron, and come freely To gratulate thy plenteous bosom: There taste, touch, all, pleased from thy table rise. They only now come but to feast thine eyes.
TIMON	They're welcome all, let 'em have kind admittance: Music, make their welcome! [*Cupid brings forward the Masquers.*]
FIRST LORD	You see, my lord, how ample you're beloved.
	[*Enter the Masquers of Amazons, with lutes in their hands, dancing and playing.*]

贵族乙	（对泰门）我们的眼睛里也因为忍不住快乐，像一个婴孩似的流起泪来了。
艾帕曼特斯	呵，呵！我一想到那个婴孩是个私生子，我就要笑死了。
贵族丙	（对泰门）大人，您使我非常感动。
艾帕曼特斯	非常感动！（喇叭奏花腔）
泰　门	那喇叭声音是怎么回事？

（一仆人上）

泰　门	什么事？
仆　人	禀大爷，有几位姑娘们在外面求见。
泰　门	姑娘们！她们来干什么？
仆　人	大爷，她们有一个领班的人，他会告诉您她们的来意。
泰　门	请她们进来吧。

（一人饰丘比特上，众舞女在其后）

丘比特	祝福你，尊贵的泰门；祝福你席上的嘉宾！人身上最灵敏的五官承认你是它们的恩主，都来向你献奉它们的珍奇。听觉、味觉、触觉、嗅觉，都已经从你的筵席上得到满足了；现在我们还要略呈薄技，贡献你视觉上的欢娱。
泰　门	欢迎欢迎；请她们进来吧。音乐，奏起来欢迎她们！

（丘比特带众舞女上）

贵族甲	大人，您看，您是这样被人敬爱。

（众女身着武士装上，手持琵琶，且弹且舞）

APEMANTUS	Hoyday, what a sweep of vanity comes this way!
	They dance? They are madwomen.
	Like madness is the glory of this life
	As this pomp shows to a little oil and root.
	We make ourselves fools to disport ourselves,
	And spend our flatteries, to drink those men
	Upon whose age we void it up again
	With poisonous spite and envy.
	Who lives that's not depravèd or depraves?
	Who dies that bears not one spurn to their graves
	Of their friends' gift?
	I should fear those that dance before me now
	Would one day stamp upon me. 'T'as been done:
	Men shut their doors against a setting sun.
	[*The Lords rise from table, with much adoring of Timon, and to show their loves each single out an Amazon, and all dance, men with women, a lofty strain or two to the hautboys, and cease.*]
TIMON	You have done our pleasures much grace, fair ladies,
	Set a fair fashion on our entertainment,
	Which was not half so beautiful and kind:
	You have added worth unto't and lustre,
	And entertained me with mine own device.
	I am to thank you for't.
FIRST LADY	My lord, you take us even at the best.
APEMANTUS	Faith, for the worst is filthy, and would not hold taking, I doubt me.
TIMON	Ladies, there is an idle banquet attends you:
	Please you to dispose yourselves.

艾帕曼特斯 哎哟！瞧这些过眼的浮华！她们跳舞！她们都是些疯婆子。人生的荣华不过是一场疯狂的胡闹，正像这种奢侈的景象在一个嚼着淡菜根的人看来一样。我们寻欢作乐，全然是傻子的行为。我们所谄媚的、我们所举杯祝饮的那些人，也就是在年老时被我们痛骂的那些人。哪一个人不曾被人败坏也败坏过别人？哪一个人死了能够逃过他的朋友的讥斥？我怕现在在我面前跳舞的人，有一天将要把我放在他们的脚下践踏；这样的事不是不曾有过，人们对于一个没落的太阳是会闭门不纳的。

（众贵族起身离席，向泰门备献殷勤；每人各择舞女一人共舞，高音笛奏闹乐一二曲；舞止）

泰　　门 各位美人，你们替我们添加了不少兴致，我们今天的欢娱，因为有了你们而格外美丽热烈了。我必须谢谢你们。

舞　女　甲 大爷，您太抬举我们了。

艾帕曼特斯 的确，不抬举就是压低，我怕那样便弄得不成体统了。

泰　　门 姑娘们，还有一桌酒席空着等候你们；请你们随意坐下吧。

ALL LADIES	Most thankfully, my lord.
	[*Cupid and Ladies Exeunt.*]
TIMON	Flavius.
FLAVIUS	My lord.
TIMON	The little casket bring me hither.
FLAVIUS	Yes, my lord. [*Aside.*] —More jewels yet!
	There is no crossing him in's humour,
	Else I should tell him well — i'faith I should —
	When all's spent, he'd be crossed then, an he could.
	'Tis pity bounty had not eyes behind,
	That man might ne'er be wretched for his mind. [*Exit.*]
FIRST LORD	Where be our men?
SERVANT	Here, my lord, in readiness.
SECOND LORD	Our horses.
	[*Enter Flavius carrying the casket.*]
TIMON	O, my friends,
	I have one word to say to you: look you, my good lord,
	[*Gives a jewel frem the casket.*] I must entreat you
	honour me so much
	As to advance this jewel. Accept it and wear it,
	Kind my lord.
FIRST LORD	I am so far already in your gifts —
ALL	So are we all. [*Timon gives jewels to all.*]
	[*Enter a Servant.*]
SERVANT	My lord, there are certain nobles of the senate
	Newly alighted and come to visit you.
TIMON	They are fairly welcome. [*Exit Servant.*]
FLAVIUS	I beseech your honour,
	Vouchsafe me a word: it does concern you near.

众　　女　谢谢大爷。

　　　　　（丘比特及众女下）

泰　　门　弗莱维斯！

弗莱维斯　有，大爷。

泰　　门　把我那小匣子拿来。

弗莱维斯　是，大爷。（旁白）又要把珠宝送人了！他高兴的时候，谁也不能违拗他的意志，否则我早就老老实实告诉他了；真的，我该早点儿告诉他，等到他把一切挥霍干净以后，再要跟他闹别扭也来不及了。可惜宽宏大量的人，背后不多生一个眼睛；心肠太好的结果不过害了自己。（下）

贵族甲　我们的仆人呢？

仆　　人　有，大爷，在这儿。

贵族乙　套起马来！

　　　　　（弗莱维斯携匣重上）

泰　　门　啊，我的朋友们！我还要对你们说一句话。（递过一颗取回珠宝匣的宝石）大人，我要请您赏我一个面子，接受了我这一颗宝石；请您收下戴上吧，我的好大人。

贵族甲　我已经得到您太多的厚赐了——

众　　人　我们也都是屡蒙见惠。（泰门向众人递过宝石）

　　　　　（仆人甲上）

仆　　甲　大爷，有几位元老院的老爷刚才到来，要来拜访。

泰　　门　我很欢迎他们。（仆人甲下）

弗莱维斯　大爷，请您让我向您说句话；那是对于您有切身关系的。

TIMON	Near? Why then, another time I'll hear thee.
	I prithee, let's be provided to show them entertainment.
FLAVIUS	[*Aside.*] I scarce know how.
	[*Enter another Servant.*]
SECOND SERVANT	May it please your honour, Lord Lucius —
	Out of his free love — hath presented to you
	Four milk-white horses trapped in silver.
TIMON	I shall accept them fairly. Let the presents
	Be worthily entertained.
	[*Exit second Servant. Enter a third Servant.*]
	How now? What news?
THIRD SERVANT	Please you, my lord, that honourable gentleman,
	Lord Lucullus, entreats your company tomorrow to
	hunt with him, and has sent your honour two brace of
	greyhounds.
TIMON	I'll hunt with him, and let them be received
	Not without fair reward.
	[*Exit third Servant.*]
FLAVIUS	[*Aside.*] What will this come to?
	He commands us to provide, and give great gifts,
	And all out of an empty coffer:
	Nor will he know his purse, or yield me this,
	To show him what a beggar his heart is,
	Being of no power to make his wishes good.
	His promises fly so beyond his state
	That what he speaks is all in debt, he owes
	For ev'ry word: he is so kind that he now
	Pays interest for't; his land's put to their books.
	Well, would I were gently put out of office

泰　　门　有切身关系！好，那么等会儿你再告诉我吧。请你快去预备预备，不要怠慢了客人。

弗莱维斯　（旁白）我简直不知道应该怎么办。

（仆人乙上）

仆　　乙　禀大爷，路歇斯大爷送来了四匹乳白的骏马，鞍辔完全是银的，要请您鉴纳他的诚意，把它们收下。

泰　　门　我很高兴接受它们；把马儿好生饲养着。（仆人乙下，仆人丙上）

啊！什么事？

仆　　丙　禀大爷，那位尊贵的绅士，路库勒斯大爷，请您明天去陪他打猎；他送来了两对猎犬。

泰　　门　我愿意陪他打猎；把猎犬收下了，用一份厚礼答谢他。

（仆人丙下）

弗莱维斯　（旁白）这样下去怎么得了呢？他命令我们预备这样预备那样，把贵重的礼物拿去送人，可是他的钱箱里却早已空得不剩一文。他又从来不想知道他究竟有多少钱，也不让我有机会告诉他实在的情形，使他知道他的力量已经不能实现他的愿望。他所答应人家的，远超过他自己的资力，因此他口头所说的每一句话都是一笔负债。他是这样的慷慨，他现在送给人家的礼物，都是他出了利息向人借贷来的；他的土地都已经抵押

	Before I were forced out.
	Happier is he that has no friend to feed
	Than such that do e'en enemies exceed.
	I bleed inwardly for my lord. [*Exit.*]
TIMON	[*To the Lords.*] You do yourselves
	Much wrong, you bate too much of your own merits.
	Here, my lord, a trifle of our love. [*Gives a gift to second Lord.*]
SECOND LORD	With more than common thanks I will receive it.
THIRD LORD	O, he's the very soul of bounty!
TIMON	[*To first Lord.*] And now I remember, my lord, you gave
	Good words the other day of a bay courser
	I rode on. 'Tis yours, because you liked it.
THIRD LORD	O, I beseech you pardon me, my lord, in that.
TIMON	You may take my word, my lord: I know, no man
	Can justly praise but what he does affect.
	I weigh my friend's affection with mine own,
	I'll tell you true. I'll call to you.
ALL LORDS	O, none so welcome.
TIMON	I take all and your several visitations
	So kind to heart, 'tis not enough to give:
	Methinks I could deal kingdoms to my friends,
	And ne'er be weary. — Alcibiades,
	Thou art a soldier, therefore seldom rich.
	[*Gives a gift.*] It comes in charity to thee, for all thy living
	Is 'mongst the dead, and all the lands thou hast
	Lie in a pitched field.

出去了。唉,但愿他早一点辞歇了我,免得将来有被迫解职的一日!与其用酒食供养这些比仇敌还凶恶的朋友,那么还是没有朋友的人幸福得多了。我在为我的主人衷心泣血呢。(下)

泰　　门　(对众贵族)你们这样自谦,真是太客气了。大人,这一点点小东西,聊以表示我们的情谊。

贵　族　乙　那么我拜领了,非常感谢。

贵　族　丙　啊,他真是个慷慨仁厚的人。

泰　　门　(对贵族甲)我记起来了,大人,前天您曾经赞美过我所乘的一匹栗色的马儿;您既然喜欢它,就把它带去吧。

贵　族　丙　啊!原谅我,大人,那我可万万不敢掠爱。

泰　　门　您尽管收下吧,大人;我知道一个人倘不是真心喜欢一样东西,决不会把它赞美得恰如其分。凭着我自己的心理,就可以推测到我的朋友的感情。我叫他们把它牵来给您。

众　贵　族　啊!那好极了。

泰　　门　承你们各位光临,我心里非常感激,即使把我的一切送给你们,也不能报答你们的盛情;我想要是我有许多国土可以分给我的朋友们,我一定永远不会感到厌倦。艾西巴第斯,你是一个军人,军人总是身无长物的,钱财难得会到你的手里(递过一份礼物);因为你的生活是与死为邻,你所有的土地都在疆场之上。

ALCIBIADES	Ay, defiled land, my lord.
FIRST LORD	We are so virtuously bound —
TIMON	And so am I to you.
THIRD LORD	So infinitely endeared —
TIMON	[*Calls.*] All to you. — Lights, more lights!
FIRST LORD	The best of happiness,
	Honour and fortunes keep with you, Lord Timon!
TIMON	Ready for his friends.

[*Exeunt Lords. Apemantus and Timon remain.*]

APEMANTUS What a coil's here,
Serving of becks and jutting-out of bums!
I doubt whether their legs be worth the sums
That are given for 'em. Friendship's full of dregs:
Methinks false hearts should never have sound legs,
Thus honest fools lay out their wealth on curtsies.

TIMON Now, Apemantus, if thou wert not sullen I would be good to thee.

APEMANTUS No, I'll nothing; for if I should be bribed too, there would be none left to rail upon thee, and then thou wouldst sin the faster. Thou giv'st so long, Timon, I fear me thou wilt give away thyself in paper shortly. What needs these feasts, pomps and vainglories?

TIMON Nay, an you begin to rail on society once, I am sworn not to give regard to you. Farewell, and come with better music. [*Exit.*]

APEMANTUS So:
Thou wilt not hear me now, thou shalt not then.
I'll lock thy heaven from thee.
O, that men's ears should be
To counsel deaf, but not to flattery! [*Exit.*]

雅典的泰门
TIMON OF ATHENS

艾西巴第斯　是的,大人,只是一些荆榛瓦砾之场。
贵　族　甲　我们深感大德——
泰　　　门　(呼唤)我也同样感谢你们。
贵　族　丙　备蒙雅爱——
泰　　　门　我也多承各位不弃。多拿些火把来!
贵　族　甲　最大的幸福、尊荣和富贵跟您在一起,泰门大人!
泰　　　门　这一切他都愿意和朋友们分享。(艾西巴第斯及贵族等同下)
艾帕曼特斯　好热闹!这么摇头晃脑撅屁股的!他们的两条腿恐怕还不值得他们跑这一趟所得到的代价。友谊不过是些渣滓废物,虚伪的心不会有坚硬的腿,老实的傻瓜们也在人们的打躬作揖之下卖弄自己的家私了。
泰　　　门　艾帕曼特斯,倘然你不是这样乖僻,我也会给你好处的。
艾帕曼特斯　不,我不要什么;要是我也受了你的贿赂,那么再也没有人骂你了,你就要造更多的孽了。你老是布施人家,泰门,我怕你快要写起卖身文契来,把你自己也送给人家了。这种宴会、奢侈、浮华是做什么用的?
泰　　　门　哎哟,要是你骂起我的交际来,那我可要发誓不理你了。再会;下次来的时候,请你预备一些好一点的音乐。(下)
艾帕曼特斯　好,你现在不要听我,将来要听也听不到了,天堂的门已经锁上了,你从此只好徘徊门外。唉,人们的耳朵不能容纳忠言,谄媚却这样容易进去!(下)

Act II

SCENE I *Athens. A Room in a Senator's House.*

[*Enter a Senator with bonds in his hand.*]

SENATOR And late, five thousand: to Varro and to Isidore
He owes nine thousand, besides my former sum,
Which makes it five-and-twenty. Still in motion
Of raging waste? It cannot hold, it will not.
If I want gold, steal but a beggar's dog
And give it Timon, why, the dog coins gold.
If I would sell my horse, and buy twenty more
Better than he, why, give my horse to Timon,
Ask nothing, give it him, it foals me straight
And able horses. No porter at his gate,
But rather one that smiles and still invites
All that pass by. It cannot hold: no reason
Can sound his state in safety. Caphis, ho!
Caphis, I say!

[*Enter Caphis.*]

CAPHIS Here, sir. What is your pleasure?
SENATOR Get on your cloak, and haste you to Lord Timon.
Importune him for my moneys. Be not ceased
With slight denial, nor then silenced when
'Commend me to your master', and the cap
Plays in the right hand, thus: but tell him
My uses cry to me, I must serve my turn

第 二 幕

第一场　雅典。某元老家中一室

（某元老手持文件上）

元　　老　最近又是五千；欠凡罗和艾西铎各九千；加上以前的旧债，前后一共是两万五千。他还在任意挥霍！这样子是维持不下去的；一定维持不下去。要是我要金子，我只要从一个乞丐那里偷一条狗送给泰门，这条狗就会替我变出金子来。要是我要把我的马卖掉，再去买二十匹比它更好的马来，我只要把我的马送给泰门，不必问他要什么。就这么送给他，它就会立刻替我生下二十匹好马来。他门口的管门人，见了谁都笑脸相迎，每一个路过的人，他都邀请他们进去。这样子是维持不下去的；他这份家私看起来恐怕有些不稳。凯菲斯，喂！凯菲斯，叫你呢！

（凯菲斯上）

凯 菲 斯　有，老爷；您有什么吩咐？

元　　老　披上你的外套，赶快到泰门大爷家里去；请他务必把我的钱还我；不要听他推三托四，也不要因为他说了一声"替我问候你家老爷"，把他的帽子放在右手这么一挥，就说不出一句话来；你要对他说，我有很要紧的用途；我必须用我自己的钱供给我自己的需要；

	Out of mine own, his days and times are past
	And my reliances on his fracted dates
	Have smit my credit. I love and honour him,
	But must not break my back to heal his finger.
	Immediate are my needs, and my relief
	Must not be tossed and turned to me in words,
	But find supply immediate. Get you gone.
	Put on a most importunate aspect,
	A visage of demand, for I do fear
	When every feather sticks in his own wing,
	Lord Timon will be left a naked gull,
	Which flashes now a phoenix. Get you gone.
CAPHIS	I go, sir.
SENATOR	'I go, sir'? Take the bonds along with you,
	[*Gives the bonds.*]
	And have the dates in. Come.
CAPHIS	I will, sir.
SENATOR	Go. [*Exeunt.*]

SCENE II *The Same. A Hall in Timon's House.*

[*Enter Steward Flavius, with many bills in his hand.*]

FLAVIUS No care, no stop: so senseless of expense
That he will neither know how to maintain it,
Nor cease his flow of riot, takes no account
How things go from him, nor resumes no care
Of what is to continue. Never mind

		他的借款早已过期，他因为爽约，我对他也失去信任了。我虽然很看重他的为人，可是不能为了医治他的手指而打伤了我自己的背；我的需要很急迫，不能让他用空话敷衍过去，一定要他立刻把钱还我。你去吧；装出一副很严厉的神气向他追索。我怕泰门大爷现在虽然像一只神采翩跹的凤凰，要是把他借来的羽毛一根根拔去以后，就要变成一只秃羽的海鸥了。你去吧。
凯 菲 斯		（递过借据）我就去，老爷。
元 老		"我就去，老爷！"把借票一起带去，别忘记借票上面的日子。
凯 菲 斯		是，老爷。
元 老		去吧。（各下）

第二场　同前。泰门家中的厅堂

（弗莱维斯持多张债票上）

弗莱维斯	他一点也不在乎，一点都不知道停止他的挥霍！不想想这样浪费下去，怎么维持得了；钱财产业从他手里飞了出去，他也不管；将来怎么过日子，他也从不放在心上；只是这样傻头傻脑地乐善好施。怎么办才好

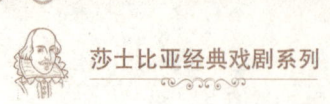

Was to be so unwise, to be so kind.
What shall be done? He will not hear, till feel.
I must be round with him, now he comes from hunting.
Fie, fie, fie, fie!

[*Enter Caphis, meeting Servants of Isidore and Varro.*]

CAPHIS Good even, Varro. What, you come for money?

VARRO'S SERVANT Is't not your business too?

CAPHIS It is: and yours too, Isidore?

ISIDORE'S SERVANT It is so.

CAPHIS Would we were all discharged!

VARRO'S SERVANT I fear it.

CAPHIS Here comes the lord.

[*Enter Timon and his train including Alcibiades.*]

TIMON So soon as dinner's done, we'll forth again,
My Alcibiades [*To Caphis.*] — With me? What is your will?

CAPHIS [*Gives a bill.*] My lord, here is a note of certain dues.

TIMON Dues? Whence are you?

CAPHIS Of Athens here, my lord.

TIMON Go to my steward.

CAPHIS Please it your lordship, he hath put me off
To the succession of new days this month:
My master is awaked by great occasion
To call upon his own, and humbly prays you
That with your other noble parts you'll suit
In giving him his right.

TIMON Mine honest friend,
I prithee but repair to me next morning.

CAPHIS Nay, good my lord —

呢？不叫他亲自尝到财尽囊空的滋味，他是再也不会听人家的话的。现在他出去打猎，快要回来了，我必须提醒他才是。嘿！嘿！嘿！嘿！

（凯菲斯及艾西铎、凡罗二家仆人上）

凯　菲　斯　晚安，凡罗家的大哥。什么！你是来讨债的吗？
凡罗家仆人　你不也是来讨债的吗？
凯　菲　斯　是的；你也是吗，艾西铎家的大哥？
艾西铎家仆人　正是。
凯　菲　斯　但愿我们都能讨到手！
凡罗家仆人　我怕有点讨不到。
凯　菲　斯　大爷来了！

（泰门、艾西巴第斯及贵族等上）

泰　　　门　我们吃过了饭再出去，艾西巴第斯。（对凯菲斯）你们是来看我的吗？有什么事？
凯　菲　斯　（递过一借据）大爷，这儿是一张债票。
泰　　　门　债票！你是哪儿来的？
凯　菲　斯　我就是这儿雅典的人，大爷。
泰　　　门　跟我的管家说去。
凯　菲　斯　禀大爷，他叫我等几天再来，可是我家主人因为自己有急用，并且知道大爷一向为人正直，千万莫让他今天失望了。
泰　　　门　我的好朋友，请你明天来吧。
凯　菲　斯　不，我的好大爷——

TIMON	Contain thyself, good friend.
VARRO'S SERVANT	One Varro's servant, my good lord —
ISIDORE'S SERVANT	From Isidore:
	He humbly prays your speedy payment.
CAPHIS	If you did know, my lord, my master's wants—
VARRO'S SERVANT	'Twas due on forfeiture, my lord, six weeks and past.
ISIDORE'S SERVANT	Your steward puts me off, my lord, and I
	Am sent expressly to your lordship.
TIMON	Give me breath. —
	[*To his train.*] I do beseech you, good my lords, keep on:
	I'll wait upon you instantly. —
	[*Exeunt Alcibiades and Lords.*]
	Come hither, Pray you, [*To Flavius.*]
	How goes the world that I am thus encountered
	With clamorous demands of broken bonds
	And the detention of long-since-due debts,
	Against my honour?
FLAVIUS	[*To Servants.*] Please you, gentlemen,
	The time is unagreeable to this business:
	Your importunacy cease till after dinner,
	That I may make his lordship understand
	Wherefore you are not paid.
TIMON	[*To Servants.*] Do so, my friends. —
	[*To Flavius.*] See them well entertained. [*Exit.*]
FLAVIUS	Pray, draw near. [*Exit. The Servants start.*]
	[*Enter Apemantus and Fool. To follow.*]
CAPHIS	Stay, stay, here comes the fool with Apemantus: Let's ha'some sport with 'em.

泰　　门　你放心吧，好朋友。
凡罗家仆人　大爷，我是凡罗的仆人——
艾西铎家仆人　艾西铎叫我来请大爷快一点把他的钱还了。
凯　菲　斯　大爷，要是您知道我家主人是怎样等着用这笔钱——
凡罗家仆人　这笔钱，大爷，已经过期六个星期了。
艾西铎家仆人　大爷，您那位管家尽是今天推明天，明天推后天的，所以我家主人才叫我向您大爷面讨。
泰　　门　让我松一口气。（对众贵族）各位大人，请你们先进去一会儿；我立刻就来奉陪。（艾西巴第斯及贵族等下）过来。请问你，（向弗莱维斯）究竟是怎么一回事，这些人都拿着过期的债票向我缠扰不清，让人家看着把我的脸也丢尽了？

（艾西巴第斯及贵族等上）

弗莱维斯　（对众仆人）对不起，各位朋友，现在不是讲这种事情的时候，请你们暂时忍耐片刻，等大爷吃过饭以后，我可以告诉他为什么你们的债款还没有归还的缘故。
泰　　门　（对众仆人）等一等再说吧，我的朋友们。（对弗莱维斯）好好地招待他们。（下，众仆人起身跟随）
弗莱维斯　请各位过来。（下）

（艾帕曼特斯及弄人上）

凯　菲　斯　且慢，瞧那傻子跟着艾帕曼特斯来了；让我们跟他们开开玩笑。

VARRO'S SERVANT	Hang him, he'll abuse us.
ISIDORE'S SERVANT	A plague upon him, dog!
VARRO'S SERVANT	How dost, fool?
APEMANTUS	Dost dialogue with thy shadow?
VARRO'S SERVANT	I speak not to thee.
APEMANTUS	No, 'tis to thyself. [*To Fool.*] — Come away.
ISIDORET'S SERVANT	[*To Varro Servant.*] There's the fool hangs on your back already.
APEMANTUS	No, thou stand'st single: thou'rt not on him yet.
CAPHIS	Where's the fool now?
APEMANTUS	He last asked the question. Poor rogues and usurers' men, bawds between gold and want.
ALL SERVANTS	What are we, Apemantus?
APEMANTUS	Asses.
ALL SERVANTS	Why?
APEMANTUS	That you ask me what you are, and do not know yourselves. Speak to 'em, fool.
FOOL	How do you, gentlemen?
ALL SERVANTS	Gramercies, good fool. How does your mistress?
FOOL	She's e'en setting on water to scald such chickens as you are. Would we could see you at Corinth!
APEMANTUS	Good, gramercy.
	[*Enter Page.*]
FOOL	Look you, here comes my master's page.
PAGE	[*To the Fool.*] Why, how now, captain? What do you in this wise company? — How dost thou, Apemantus?
APEMANTUS	Would I had a rod in my mouth, that I might answer thee profitably.

凡罗家仆人	别理他，他会骂我们的。
艾西铎家仆人	该死的狗！
凡罗家仆人	你好，傻子？
艾帕曼特斯	你在对你的影子讲话吗？
凡罗家仆人	我不是跟你说话。
艾帕曼特斯	不，你是对你自己说话。（向弄人）去吧。
艾西铎家仆人	（向凡罗家仆人）傻子已经附在你的背上了。
艾帕曼特斯	不对，你只是一个人站在那里，还没有骑上他的背呢。
凯菲斯	此刻那傻子呢？
艾帕曼特斯	问这问题的就是那傻子。哼，这些放债人手下的奴才！都是些金钱与欲望之间的娼家。
众　仆	我们是什么，艾帕曼特斯？
艾帕曼特斯	都是些驴子。
众　仆	为什么？
艾帕曼特斯	因为你们不知道自己是什么，却要来问我。跟他们谈谈，傻子。
弄　人	各位请了。
众　仆	你好，好傻子。你家奶奶好吗？
弄　人	她正在烧开热水来替你们这些小鸡洗皮拔毛哩。巴不得在妓院里看到你们！
艾帕曼特斯	说得好！
	（侍童上）
弄　人	瞧，咱们奶奶的童儿来了。
侍　童	（向弄人）啊，您好，大将军！您在这些聪明人中间有什么贵干？你好，艾帕曼特斯？
艾帕曼特斯	我但愿我的舌头上长着一根棒儿，可以痛痛快快地回答你。

PAGE [*Gives letters.*] Prithee, Apemantus, read me the superscription of these letters: I know not which is which.

APEMANTUS Canst not read?

PAGE No.

APEMANTUS There will little learning die then, that day thou art hanged. This is to Lord Timon, this to Alcibiades. Go, thou wast born a bastard, and thou'lt die a bawd.

PAGE Thou wast whelped a dog, and thou shalt famish a dog's death. Answer not, I am gone. [*Exit.*]

APEMANTUS E'en so thou outrunn'st grace.—
Fool, I will go with you to Lord Timon's.

FOOL Will you leave me there?

APEMANTUS If Timon stay at home. [*To Servants.*] — You three serve three usurers?

ALL SERVANTS Ay: would they served us!

APEMANTUS So would I: as good a trick as ever hangman served thief.

FOOL Are you three usurers' men?

ALL SERVANTS Ay, fool.

FOOL I think no usurer but has a fool to his servant: my mistress is one, and I am her fool. When men come to borrow of your masters, they approach sadly and go away merry, but they enter my master's house merrily and go away sadly: the reason of this?

VARRO'S SERVANT I could render one.

APEMANTUS Do it then, that we may account thee a whoremaster and a knave, which notwithstanding thou shalt be no less esteemed.

VARRO'S SERVANT What is a whoremaster, fool?

侍　　童	（递过信）艾帕曼特斯，请你把这两个信封上的字念给我听一听，我不知道哪一封信应该给哪一个人。
艾帕曼特斯	你不认识字吗？
侍　　童	不认识。
艾帕曼特斯	那么你吊死的一天，学问倒不会受损失了。这是给泰门大爷的；这是给艾西巴第斯的。去吧；你生下来是个私生子，到死是个忘八蛋。
侍　　童	母狗把你生了下来，你死了也是一条饿狗。不要回答我，我去了。（童下）
艾帕曼特斯	好，你夹着尾巴逃吧。——傻瓜，我要跟你一块儿到泰门大爷那儿去。
弄　　人	您要把我丢在那儿吗？
艾帕曼特斯	要是泰门在家，我就把你丢在那儿。（对众仆人）你们三个人侍候着三个放债的人吗？
众　　仆	是的；我们但愿他们侍候我们！
艾帕曼特斯	那倒跟刽子手侍候偷儿一样好玩。
弄　　人	你们三个人的主人都是放债的吗？
众　　仆	是的，傻瓜。
弄　　人	我想是个放债的就得有个傻瓜做他的仆人；我家奶奶是个放债的，我就是她的傻瓜。人家向你们的主人借钱，来的时候都是愁眉苦脸，去的时候都是欢欢喜喜；可是人家走进我家奶奶的屋子的时候，却是欢欢喜喜，走出去的时候反而愁眉苦脸，这是什么道理呢？
凡罗家仆人	我可以说出一个道理来。
艾帕曼特斯	那么你说吧，你说了出来，我们就可以承认你是一个忘八龟子，虽然你本来就是个忘八龟子。
凡罗家仆人	傻瓜，什么叫忘八龟子？

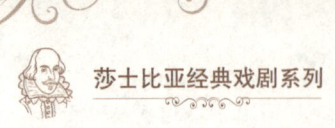

FOOL	A fool in good clothes, and something like thee. 'Tis a spirit: sometime't appears like a lord, sometime like a lawyer, sometime like a philosopher with two stones more than's artificial one. He is very often like a knight; and generally in all shapes that man goes up and down in from fourscore to thirteen, this spirit walks in.
VARRO'S SERVANT	Thou art not altogether a fool.
FOOL	Nor thou altogether a wise man: as much foolery as I have, so much wit thou lack'st.
APEMANTUS	That answer might have become Apemantus.
ALL SERVANTS	Aside, aside, here comes Lord Timon.

[*Enter Timon and Steward.*]

APEMANTUS	Come with me, fool, come.
FOOL	I do not always follow lover, elder brother and woman: sometime the philosopher.

[*Exeunt Apemantus and Fool.*]

FLAVIUS	Pray you walk near: I'll speak with you anon.

[*Exeunt Servants.*]

TIMON	You make me marvel wherefore ere this time Had you not fully laid my state before me, That I might so have rated my expense As I had leave of means?
FLAVIUS	You would not hear me: At many leisures I proposed.
TIMON	Go to: Perchance some single vantages you took When my indisposition put you back, And that unaptness made your minister Thus to excuse yourself.

弄　　　人	他是一个穿着好衣服的傻瓜,跟你差不多的一种东西。是一个鬼魂:有时候样子像一个贵人;有时候像一个律师;有时候像一个哲学家,系着两颗天生的药丸;又往往以一个骑士的姿态出现;这个鬼魂也会化成各色各样的人,有时候是个八十岁的老头儿,有时候是个十三岁的小哥儿。
凡罗家仆人	你倒不完全是个傻子。
弄　　　人	你也不完全是个聪明人;我不过有几分傻气,你也刚刚缺少这几分聪明。
艾帕曼特斯	这倒像是艾帕曼特斯说的话。
众　　　仆	站开,站开;泰门大爷来了。
	(泰门及弗莱维斯重上)
艾帕曼特斯	跟我来,傻瓜,来。
弄　　　人	我不大愿意跟在情人、长兄和女人的背后;有时候也不愿意跟着哲学家跑。(艾帕曼特斯及弄人下)
弗莱维斯	请您过来:我一会儿就跟你们说话。(众仆下)
泰　　　门	你真使我奇怪;为什么你不早一点把我的家用收支的情形明白告诉我,好让我在没有欠债以前,把费用节省节省呢?
弗莱维斯	我好几回向您说起,您总是不理会我。
泰　　　门	哼,也许你趁着我心里不高兴的时候说起这种话,我叫你不要向我絮烦,你就借着这个做理由,替你自己诿卸责任了。

莎士比亚经典戏剧系列

FLAVIUS	O my good lord,
	At many times I brought in my accounts,
	Laid them before you: you would throw them off,
	And say, you found them in mine honesty.
	When for some trifling present you have bid me
	Return so much, I have shook my head and wept:
	Yea, gainst th'authority of manners prayed you
	To hold your hand more close. I did endure
	Not seldom, nor no slight checks when I have
	Prompted you in the ebb of your estate
	And your great flow of debts. My lovèd lord,
	Though you hear now too late, yet now's a time:
	The greatest of your having lacks a half
	To pay your present debts.
TIMON	Let all my land be sold.
FLAVIUS	'Tis all engaged, some forfeited and gone,
	And what remains will hardly stop the mouth
	Of present dues. The future comes apace:
	What shall defend the interim, and at length
	How goes our reck'ning?
TIMON	To Lacedaemon did my land extend.
FLAVIUS	O, my good lord, the world is but a word:
	Were it all yours to give it in a breath,
	How quickly were it gone!
TIMON	You tell me true.
FLAVIUS	If you suspect my husbandry or falsehood,
	Call me before th'exactest auditors
	And set me on the proof. So the gods bless me,
	When all our offices have been oppressed

弗莱维斯	啊,我的好大爷!好多次我把账目拿上来呈给您看,您总是把它们推在一旁,说是您相信我的忠实。当您收下了人家一点点轻微的礼品,叫我用许多贵重的东西酬答他们的时候,我总是摇头流泪,甚至于不顾自己卑贱的身份,再三劝告您不要太慷慨了。不止一次我因为向您指出您的财产已经大不如前,您的欠债已经愈积愈多,而您却对我严词申斥。我的亲爱的大爷,现在您虽然肯听我把实在的情形告诉您,可是已经太迟了,您的家产至多也不过抵偿您的欠债的半数。
泰 门	把我的土地一起卖掉好了。
弗莱维斯	土地有的已经变卖了,有的已经抵押给人家了;剩下来的还不够偿还目前已经到期的债款;没有到期的债款也快要到期了,中间这一段时间怎么应付过去呢?我们这一笔账,到最后又是怎么算法?
泰 门	我的土地不是一直通到斯巴达吗?
弗莱维斯	啊,我的好大爷!整个的世界也不过是一句话;即使它是完全属于您的,只要您一开口,也可以把它很快地送给别人。
泰 门	你说的倒是真话。
弗莱维斯	要是您疑心我办事欺心,您可以叫几个最精细的查账员当面查看我的账目。神明在上,当我们的门庭之内充满着饕餮的食客,当我们的酒窟里泛滥着满地的余

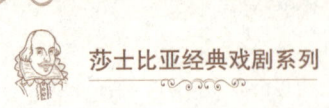

	With riotous feeders, when our vaults have wept
	With drunken spilth of wine, when every room
	Hath blazed with lights and brayed with minstrelsy,
	I have retired me to a wasteful cock,
	And set mine eyes at flow.
TIMON	Prithee, no more.
FLAVIUS	Heavens, have I said, the bounty of this lord!
	How many prodigal bits have slaves and peasants
	This night englutted! Who is not Timon's?
	What heart, head, sword, force, means, but is
	Lord Timon's?
	Great Timon, noble, worthy, royal Timon!
	Ah, when the means are gone that buy this praise,
	The breath is gone whereof this praise is made:
	Feast-won, fast-lost; one cloud of winter show'rs,
	These flies are couched.
TIMON	Come, sermon me no further:
	No villainous bounty yet hath passed my heart;
	Unwisely, not ignobly, have I given.
	Why dost thou weep? Canst thou the conscience lack,
	To think I shall lack friends? Secure thy heart:
	If I would broach the vessels of my love
	And try the argument of hearts by borrowing,
	Men and men's fortunes could I frankly use
	As I can bid thee speak.
FLAVIUS	Assurance bless your thoughts!
TIMON	And in some sort these wants of mine are crowned
	That I account them blessings, for by these
	Shall I try friends: you shall perceive how you

沥，当每一间屋内灯光吐辉，笙歌沸天的时候，我总是一个人躲在一个漏水的管子下面，止不住我的泪涛的汹涌。

泰　　门　请你不要说下去啦。

弗莱维斯　天啊！我总是说，这位大爷多么慷慨！在这一个晚上，有多少狼藉的酒肉填饱了庸奴伧夫的肠胃！哪一个人不是靠泰门养活的？哪一个人的心思才智、武力资财，不是泰门大爷的？伟大的泰门。光荣高贵的泰门，唉！花费了无数的钱财，买到人家一声赞美，钱财一旦去手，赞美的声音也寂灭了。酒食上得来的朋友，等到酒尽樽空，转眼成为路人；一片冬天的乌云刚刚出现，这些飞虫们早就躲得不知去向了。

泰　　门　得啦，少教训几句吧；我虽然太慷慨了些，可是慷慨也不是坏事；我的钱财用得虽然不大得当，可是还不是用在不明不白的地方。你何必哭呢？你难道以为我会缺少朋友吗？放心吧，凭着我对人家这点交情，要是我开口向人告借，谁都会把他们自己和他们的财产给我自由支配的。

弗莱维斯　但愿您所深信的果然是事实！

泰　　门　而且我现在的贫乏，未始不可以说是一种幸运；因为我可以借此试探我的朋友。你就可以明白你对于我的

	Mistake my fortunes. I am wealthy in my friends. — Within there, Flaminius, Servilius! [*Calls.*]
	[*Enter three Servants.*]
SERVANTS	My lord, my lord.
TIMON	I will dispatch you severally: [*To Servilius.*] you to Lord Lucius, —
	[*To Flaminius.*] to Lord Lucullus you —I hunted with his honour today — [*To Third Servant.*] you to Sempronius. Commend me to their loves, and I am proud, say, that my occasions have found time to use 'em toward a supply of money: let the request be fifty talents.
FLAMINIUS	As you have said, my lord.
FLAVIUS	[*Aside.*] Lord Lucius and Lucullus? Hum!
TIMON	[*To another Servant.*] Go you, sir, to the senators — Of Whom, even to the state's best health, I have Deserved this hearing — bid 'em send o'th'instant A thousand talents to me.
FLAVIUS	I have been bold — For that I knew it the most general way — To them to use your signet and your name, But they do shake their heads, and I am here No richer in return.
TIMON	Is't true? Can't be?
FLAVIUS	They answer in a joint and corporate voice That now they are at fall, want treasure, cannot Do what they would, are sorry, you are honourable, But yet they could have wished — they know not — Something hath been amiss, a noble nature

财产的忧心完全是一种过虑，我有这许多朋友，还怕穷吗？（呼唤）里面有人吗？弗莱米涅斯！塞维律斯！

（弗莱米涅斯、塞维律斯及其他仆人上）

众　　仆　大爷！大爷！

泰　　门　你们替我分别到几个地方去：（对塞维律斯）你到路歇斯大爷那里；（对弗莱米涅斯）你到路库勒斯大爷那里，我今天还跟他在一起打猎；（对仆人丙）你到辛普洛涅斯那里。替我向他们致意问候；说是我认为非常荣幸，能够有机会请求他们借给我一些钱；只要五十个泰伦就够了。

弗莱米涅斯　是，大爷，我们就照您这几句话去说。（众仆人下）

弗莱维斯　（旁白）路歇斯和路库勒斯？哼！

泰　　门　（向另一仆人）你到元老院去，请他们立刻送一千泰伦来给我；为了国计民生我曾尽过力，现在他们也该答应我的请求。

弗莱维斯　我已经大胆用您的图章和名义，向他们请求过了；可是他们只向我摇摇头，结果我仍旧空手而归。

泰　　门　真的吗？有这种事！

弗莱维斯　他们众口一词地回答我说，现在他们的境况很困难，手头没有钱，力不从心，很抱歉；您是很有信誉的人；可是他们觉得——他们不知道；有一点儿不敢十分赞

	May catch a wrench — would all were well — 'tis pity.
	And so, intending other serious matters,
	After distasteful looks and these hard fractions,
	With certain half-caps and cold-moving nods
	They froze me into silence.
TIMON	You gods reward them!
	Prithee, man, look cheerly. These old fellows
	Have their ingratitude in them hereditary:
	Their blood is caked, 'tis cold, it seldom flows:
	'Tis lack of kindly warmth they are not kind;
	And nature, as it grows again toward earth,
	Is fashioned for the journey, dull and heavy. —
	[*To a Servant.*] Go to Ventidius. —
	[*To Flavius.*] Prithee be not sad:
	Thou art true and honest; ingeniously I speak.
	No blame belongs to thee.
	[*To Servant.*] — Ventidius lately
	Buried his father, by whose death he's stepped
	Into a great estate: when he was poor,
	Imprisoned and in scarcity of friends,
	I cleared him with five talents. Greet him from me,
	Bid him suppose some good necessity
	Touches his friend, which craves to be remembered
	With those five talents. — [*Exit Servant.*]
	[*To Flavius.*] That had, give't these fellows
	To whom 'tis instant due. Ne'er speak or think
	That Timon's fortunes 'mong his friends can sink.
FLAVIUS	I would I could not think it: that thought is bounty's foe;
	Being free itself, it thinks all others so. [*Exeunt.*]

同；善人未必没有过失；但愿一切顺利；实在不胜遗憾之至；说着这样断断续续的话，满脸不耐烦的神气，把帽子往上掀了掀，冷淡地点了点头，就去忙别的要事去了，把我冷得哑口无言。

泰　　门　神啊，惩罚他们！老人家，你不用烦恼。这些老家伙，都是天生忘恩负义的东西；他们的血已经冻结寒冷，不会流了；他们因为缺少热力，所以这样冷酷无情；他们将要终结他们生命的旅程而归于泥土，所以他们的天性也变得冥顽不灵了。（向一仆）你到文提狄斯那儿去。（向弗莱维斯）你也不用伤心了，你是忠心而诚实的；这全然不是你的错处。（向那仆人）文提狄斯新近把他的父亲安葬；他自从父亲死了以后，已经承继到一笔很大的遗产；他关在监狱里的时候，穷得一个朋友也没有，是我用五泰伦把他赎了出来；你去替我向他致意，对他说他的朋友因为有一些正用，请他把那五泰伦还给他。（仆人下。向弗莱维斯）那五泰伦拿到以后，就把目前已经到期的债款还给那些家伙。泰门有的是朋友，他的家业是不会没落的。

弗莱维斯　我希望我也像您一样放心。顾虑是慷慨的仇敌；一个人自己慷慨了，就以为人家也跟你一样。（同下）

Act III

SCENE I Athens. A Room in Lucullus' House.

[*Enter Flaminius waiting to speak with a Lord from his master, enters a Servant to him.*]

SERVANT I have told my lord of you: he is coming down to you.
FLAMINIUS I thank you, sir.
[*Enter Lucullus.*]
SERVANT Here's my lord.
LUCULLUS [*Aside.*] One of Lord Timon's men? A gift, I warrant. Why, this hits right; I dreamt of a silver basin and ewer tonight. — Flaminius, honest Flaminius, you are very respectively welcome, sir. — Fill me some wine.—[*To Servant.*] And how does that honourable, complete, free-hearted gentleman of Athens, thy very bountiful good lord and master? [*Exit Servant.*]
FLAMINIUS His health is well sir.
LUCULLUS I am right glad that his health is well,sir. And what hast thou there under thy cloak, pretty Flaminius?
FLAMINIUS Faith, nothing but an empty box, sir, which in my lord's behalf I come to entreat your honour to supply, who, having great and instant occasion to use fifty talents, hath sent to your lordship to furnish him, nothing doubting your present assistance therein.
LUCULLUS La, la, la, la! 'Nothing doubting' says he? Alas, good lord! A noble gentleman 'tis, if he would not keep so

第 三 幕

第一场 雅典。路库勒斯家中一室

（弗莱米涅斯在室中等候；一仆人上）

仆　　人　我已经告诉我家大爷说你在这儿；他就来见你了。

弗莱米涅斯　谢谢你，大哥。

（路库勒斯上）

仆　　人　这就是我家大爷。

路库勒斯　（旁白）泰门大爷的一个仆人！一定是送什么礼物来的。哈哈，一点不错；我昨天晚上梦见银盘和银瓶哩。弗莱米涅斯，好弗莱米涅斯，承蒙你光降，不胜欢迎之至。给我倒些酒来。（对仆人）那位尊贵的，十全十美的、宽宏大量的雅典绅士，你那慷慨的好主人好吗？（仆人下）

弗莱米涅斯　他身体很好，先生。

路库勒斯　我很高兴他身体很好。你那外套下面有些什么东西，可爱的弗莱米涅斯？

弗莱米涅斯　不瞒您说，先生，那不过是一只空匣子；我奉我家大爷之命，特来请您把它填满了；他因为急用，需要五十个泰伦，所以叫我来向您商借，他相信您一定会毫不踌躇地帮助他的。

路库勒斯　哪，哪，哪哪！"相信我一定会帮助他"，他这样说吗？

good a house. Many a time and often I ha' dined with him, and told him on't, and come again to supper to him of purpose to have him spend less, and yet he would embrace no counsel, take no warning by my coming. Every man has his fault, and honesty is his: I ha' told him on't, but I could ne'er get him from't.

[*Enter Servant with wine.*]

SERVANT Please your lordship, here is the wine.

LUCULLUS Flaminius, I have noted thee always wise. Here's to thee. [*Toasts.*]

FLAMINIUS Your lordship speaks your pleasure.

LUCULLUS I have observed thee always for a towardly prompt spirit, give thee thy due, and one that knows what belongs to reason; and canst use the time well, if the time use thee well. Good parts in thee.— [*To Servant.*] Get you gone, sirrah. — [*Exit Servant.*] Draw nearer, honest Flaminius. Thy lord's a bountiful gentleman; but thou art wise, and thou know'st well enough — although thou com'st to me — that this is no time to lend money, especially upon bare friendship without security. Here's three solidares for thee. Good boy, wink at me and say thou saw'st me not. Fare thee well. [*Gives money.*]

FLAMINIUS Is't possible the world should so much differ,
And we alive that lived? Fly, damnèd baseness,
To him that worships thee. [*Throws back the money.*]

LUCULLUS Ha? Now I see thou art a fool, and fit for thy master. [*Exit.*]

FLAMINIUS May these add to the number that may scald thee!

雅典的泰门
TIMON OF ATHENS

唉！好大爷，他是一位尊贵的绅士，就是太爱摆阔了。我好多次陪他在一块儿吃中饭，打算劝劝他，晚上再去陪他吃晚饭，也是为着劝他不要太浪费；可是他总不肯听人家的劝，也不因为我一次次地上门而有所觉悟。哪一个人没有几分错处，他的错处就是太老实了；我也这样对他说过，可是没有法子改变他的习性。

（仆人持酒重上）

仆　　人　大爷，酒来了。

路库勒斯　弗莱米涅斯，我一向知道你是个聪明人。喝杯酒吧。

（敬酒）

弗莱米涅斯　多承大爷谬奖。

路库勒斯　我常常注意到你的脾气很和顺勤勉，凭良心说，你是很懂得道理的；你也从来不偷懒，这些都是你的好处。（向仆人）你去吧。（仆人下）过来，好弗莱米涅斯，你家大爷是位慷慨的绅士；可是你是个聪明人，虽然你到这儿来看我，你也一定明白，现在不是可以借钱给别人的时世，尤其单单凭着一点交情，什么保证都没有，那怎么行呀？这儿有三毛钱你拿了去；好孩子，帮帮忙，就说你没有看见我就是了。再会。（递过钱）

弗莱米涅斯　世事的变迁，人情的变幻，竟会至于此吗？滚开，该死的下贱的东西，回到那崇拜你的人那儿去吧！（将钱掷去）

路库勒斯　嘿！原来你也是个傻子，这才是有其主必有其仆。（下）

弗莱米涅斯　愿你落在铁锅里和着熔化了的钱活活地熬死，你这恶

Let molten coin be thy damnation,
Thou disease of a friend, and not himself!
Has friendship such a faint and milky heart,
It turns in less than two nights? O you gods,
I feel my master's passion! This slave
Unto his honour has my lord's meat in him:
Why should it thrive and turn to nutriment,
When he is turned to poison?
O, may diseases only work upon't it!
And when he's sick to death, let not that part of nature
Which my lord paid for be of any power
To expel sickness, but prolong his hour. [*Exit.*]

SCENE II   *The Same. A public place.*

[*Enter Lucius with three Strangers.*]

LUCIUS   Who, the Lord Timon? He is my very good friend, and an honourable gentleman.

FIRST STRANGER   We know him for no less, though we are but strangers to him. But I can tell you one thing, my lord, and which I hear from common rumours: now Lord Timon's happy hours are done and past, and his estate shrinks from him.

LUCIUS   Fie, no, do not believe it: he cannot want for money.

SECOND STRANGER   But believe you this, my lord, that not long ago, one of his men was with the lord Lucullus to borrow so many talents — nay, urged extremely for't and showed what necessity belonged to't, and yet was denied.

病一样的朋友！难道友谊是这样轻浮善变，不到两天工夫就换了样子吗？天啊！我的心头充塞着我主人的愤怒。这个奴才的肠胃里还有我家主人赏给他吃的肉，为什么这些肉不跟他的良心一起变坏，化成毒药呢？他的生命一部分是靠着我家主人养活的；但愿他害起病来，临死之前多挨一些痛苦！（下）

第二场　同前。广场

（路歇斯及三路人上）

路　歇　斯　谁？泰门大爷吗？他是我的很好的朋友，也是一个高贵的绅士。

路　人　甲　我们也久闻他的大名，虽然跟他没有交情。可是我可以告诉您一件事情，我听一般人都这样纷纷传说，说现在泰门大爷的光荣时代已经过去，他的家业已经远不如前了。

路　歇　斯　嘿，哪有这样的事，你不要听信人家胡说；他是总不会缺钱的。

路　人　乙　可是您得相信我，在不久以前，他叫一个仆人到路库勒斯大爷家里去，向他告借多少泰伦，说是有很要紧的用途，可是结果并没有借到。

LUCIUS	How?
SECOND STRANGER	I tell you, denied, my lord.
LUCIUS	What a strange case was that? Now before the gods, I am ashamed on't. Denied that honourable man? There was very little honour showed in't. For my own part, I must needs confess I have received some small kindnesses from him, as money, plate, jewels and such-like trifles — nothing comparing to his: yet, had he mistook him and sent to me, I should ne'er have denied his occasion so many talents.

[*Enter Servilius.*]

SERVILIUS	[*Aside.*] See, by good hap, yonder's my lord: I have sweat to see his honour. [*To Lucius.*] — My honoured lord. —
LUCIUS	Servilius! You are kindly met, sir. Fare thee well: commend me to thy honourable virtuous lord, my very exquisite friend.
SERVILIUS	May it please your honour, my lord hath sent —
LUCIUS	Ha? What has he sent? I am so much endeared to that lord; he's ever sending: how shall I thank him, think'st thou? And what has he sent now?
SERVILIUS	Has only sent his present occasion now, my lord, requesting your lordship to supply his instant use with so many talents. [*Presents a note.*]
LUCIUS	I know his lordship is but merry with me: [*Reads the note.*] He cannot want fifty — five hundred talents!
SERVILIUS	But in the meantime he wants less, my lord.

路歇斯　　怎么!

路人乙　　我说,他没有借到。

路歇斯　　岂有此理!天神在上,我真替他害羞!不肯借钱给这样一位高贵的绅士!那真是太不讲道义了。拿我自己来说,我必须承认曾经从他手里得到过一些小恩小惠,譬如说钱哪、杯盘哪、珠宝哪,这一类零星小物,比起别人到手的东西来可比不上,可是要是他向我开口借钱,我是不会不借给他这几个泰伦的。

(塞维律斯上)

塞维律斯　(旁白)瞧,巧得很,那里正是路歇斯大爷;我好容易找到他。(向路歇斯)我的尊贵的大爷!

路歇斯　　塞维律斯!你来得很好。再会;替我问候你的高贵贤德的主人,我的最好的朋友。

塞维律斯　告诉大爷知道,我家主人叫我来——

路歇斯　　哈!他又叫你送什么东西来了吗?你家大爷待我真好,他老送东西给我;你看我应当怎样感谢他才好呢?他现在又送些什么来啦?

塞维律斯　他没有送什么来,大爷,只是因为一时需要,想请您借给他几个泰伦。(呈上一借条)

路歇斯　　我知道他老人家只是跟我开开玩笑;(读借条)他哪里会缺五十、一百个泰伦用。

塞维律斯　可是大爷,他现在需要的还不到这个数目。要是他的

	If his occasion were not virtuous,
	I should not urge it half so faithfully.
LUCIUS	Dost thou speak seriously, Servilius?
SERVILIUS	Upon my soul, 'tis true, sir.
LUCIUS	What a wicked beast was I to disfurnish myself against such a good time, when I might ha' shown myself honourable! How unluckily it happened that I should purchase the day before for a little part, and undo a great deal of honour. Servilius, now before the gods, I am not able to do — the more beast, I say— I was sending to use Lord Timon myself — these gentlemen can witness — but I would not, for the wealth of Athens, I had don't now. Commend me bountifully to his good lordship, and I hope his honour will conceive the fairest of me because I have no power to be kind: and tell him this from me, I count it one of my greatest afflictions, say, that I cannot pleasure such an honourable gentleman. Good Servilius, will you befriend me so far, as to use mine own words to him?
SERVILIUS	Yes, sir, I shall. [*Exit Servilius.*]
LUCIUS	[*Calls after him.*] I'll look you out a good turn, Servilius. —
	True as you said, Timon is shrunk indeed:
	And he that's once denied will hardly speed. [*Exit.*]
FIRST STRANGER	Do you observe this, Hostilius?
SECOND STRANGER	Ay, too well.
FIRST STRANGER	Why, this is the world's soul, and just of the same piece Is every flatterer's sport. Who can call him his friend

用途并不正当，我也不会向您这样苦苦求告的。

路歇斯　你说的是真话吗，塞维律斯？

塞维律斯　凭着我的灵魂起誓，我说的是真话。

路歇斯　我真是一头该死的畜生，放着这一个大好的机会，可以表明我自己不是一个翻脸无情的小人，偏偏把手头的钱一起用光了！真不凑巧，前天我买了一件无关重要的东西，今天蒙泰门大爷给我这样一个面子，却不能应命。塞维律斯，天神在上，我真的是无力应命；我是一头畜生；我自己刚才还想叫人来向泰门大爷告借几个钱呢，这三位先生可以替我证明的；可是我觉得不好意思，否则早就向他开口了。请你多多替我向你家大爷致意；我希望他不要见怪于我，因为我实在是心有余而力不足。再请你替我告诉他，我不能满足这样一位高贵的绅士的要求，真是我生平第一件恨事。好塞维律斯，你愿意做我的好朋友，照我这几句话对他说吗？

塞维律斯　好的，大爷，我这样对他说就是了。（塞维律斯下）

路歇斯　（在他身后呼喊）我一定不忘记你的好处，塞维律斯。你们果然说得不错，泰门已经失势了，一次被人拒绝，到处都要碰壁的。（下）

路人甲　您看见这种情形吗，霍斯提律斯？

路人乙　嗯，我看得太明白了。

路人甲　哼，这就是世人的本来面目；每一个谄媚之徒，都是同样的居心。谁能够叫那同器而食的人做他的朋友呢？

                  That dips in the same dish? For, in my knowing,
Timon has been this lord's father,
And kept his credit with his purse,
Supported his estate: nay, Timon's money
Has paid his men their wages. He ne'er drinks,
But Timon's silver treads upon his lip,
And yet — O, see the monstrousness of man
When he looks out in an ungrateful shape!—
He does deny him, in respect of his,
What charitable men afford to beggars.

THIRD STRANGER Religion groans at it.

FIRST STRANGER For mine own part,
I never tasted Timon in my life,
Nor came any of his bounties over me
To mark me for his friend: yet, I protest,
For his right noble mind, illustrious virtue
And honourable carriage,
Had his necessity made use of me
I would have put my wealth into donation,
And the best half should have returned to him,
So much I love his heart. But I perceive
Men must learn now with pity to dispense,
For policy sits above conscience. [*Exeunt.*]

雅典的泰门
TIMON OF ATHENS

据我所知道的，泰门曾经像父亲一样照顾这位贵人，用他自己的钱替他还债，维持他的产业；甚至于他的仆人的工钱，也是泰门替他代付的；他每一次喝酒，他的嘴唇上都是啜着泰门的银子；可是唉！瞧这些狗彘不食的人！人家行善事，对乞丐也要布施几个钱，他却好意思这样忘恩负义地一口拒绝。

路人丙　世道如斯，鬼神有知，亦当痛哭。

路人甲　拿我自己来说，我虽然从来不曾叨光过泰门的一顿酒食；他也从来不曾施恩于我，可以表明我是他的一个朋友；可是我要说一句，为了他的正直的胸襟、超人的德行和高贵的举止，要是他在窘迫的时候需要我的帮助，我一定愿意变卖我的家产，把一大半送给他，因为我是这样敬爱他的为人。可是在现在的时世，一个人也只好把怜悯之心搁起，因为万事总须熟权利害，不能但问良心。（同下）

SCENE III *The Same. A Room in Sempronius' House.*

[*Enter A third Servant with Sempronius, another of Timon's friends.*]

SEMPRONIUS Must he needs trouble me in't. Hum! 'Bove all others?
He might have tried Lord Lucius or Lucullus,
And now Ventidius is wealthy too,
Whom he redeemed from prison: all these
Owes their estates unto him.

SERVANT My lord,
They have all been touched and found base metal,
For they have all denied him.

SEMPRONIUS How? Have they denied him?
Has Ventidius and Lucullus denied him,
And does he send to me? Three? Hum!
It shows but little love or judgment in him.
Must I be his last refuge? His friends, like physicians,
Thrice, give him over: must I take th'cure upon me?
He's much disgraced me in't: I'm angry at him,
That might have known my place.I see no sense for't,
But his occasions might have wooed me first,
For, in my conscience, I was the first man
That e'er receivèd gift from him:
And does he think so backwardly of me now,
That I'll requite it last? No:
So it may prove an argument of laughter
To th'rest, and 'mongst lords be thought a fool.
I'd rather than the worth of thrice the sum,

第三场 同前。辛普洛涅斯家中一室

（辛普洛涅斯及一泰门的仆人上）

辛普洛涅斯 哼！难道他没有别人，一定要找我吗？他可以向路歇斯或是路库勒斯试试；文提狄斯是他从监狱里赎出身来的，现在也发了财了：这几个人都是靠着他才有今天这份财产。

仆　　人 大爷，他们几个人的地方都去过了，一个也不是好东西，谁都不肯借给他。

辛普洛涅斯 怎么！他们已经拒绝了他吗？文提狄斯和路库勒斯都拒绝了他吗？他现在又来向我告借吗？三个人？哼！这就可以看出他不但不够交情，而且也太缺少知人之明；我必须做他的最后的希望吗？他的朋友已经三次拒绝了他，就像一个病人已经被三个医生认为不治，所以我必须负责把他医好吗？他明明瞧不起我，给我这样重大的侮辱，我在生他的气哩。他应该一开始就向我商量，因为凭良心说，我是第一个收到他的礼物的人；现在他却最后一个才想到我，想叫我在最后帮他的忙吗？不，要是我答应了他，人家都要笑我，那些贵人们都要当我是个傻子了。要是他瞧得起我，第

Had sent to me first, but for my mind's sake:
I'd such a courage to do him good. But now return,
And with their faint reply this answer join:
Who bates mine honour shall not know my coin. [*Exit.*]

SERVANT Excellent. Your lordship's a goodly villain. The devil knew not what he did when he made man politic; he crossed himself by't, and I cannot think but in the end the villainies of man will set him clear. How fairly this lord strives to appear foul! Takes virtuous copies to be wicked, like those that under hot ardent zeal would set whole realms on fire: of such a nature is his politic love.

This was my lord's best hope. Now all are fled,
Save only the gods. Now his friends are dead.
Doors that were ne'er acquainted with their wards
Many a bounteous year must be employed
Now to guard sure their master.
And this is all a liberal course allows:
Who cannot keep his wealth must keep his house.
[*Exit.*]

SCENE IV   *The Same. A Hall in Timon's House.*

[*Enter Varro's men meeting others: all Timon's creditors to wait for his coming out. Then enter, a Servant of, Lucius Titus and Hortensius.*]

VARRO'S FIRST SERVANT Well met: good morrow, Titus and Hortensius.

　　　　　　一个就向我借,那么别说这一点数目,就是三倍于此,我也愿意帮助他的。可是现在你回去吧,替我把我的答复跟他们的冷淡的回音一起告诉你家主人;谁轻视了我,休想用我的钱。(下)

仆　人　很好!你这位大爷也是一个大大的奸徒。魔鬼把人们造得这样奸诈,一定后悔无及;比起人心的险恶来,魔鬼也要望风却步哩。瞧这位贵人唯恐人家看不清楚他的丑恶,拼命龇牙咧嘴给人家看,这就是他的奸诈的友谊!这是我的主人的最后的希望;现在一切都已消失了,只有向神明祈祷。现在他的朋友都已死去;终年开放、来者不拒的大门,也要关起来保护它们的主人了;这是一个浪子的下场;一个人不能看守住他的家产,就只好关起大门躲债。(下)

第四场　同前。泰门家中厅堂

(凡罗家两个仆人及路歇斯的仆人同上,与泰特斯、霍坦歇斯及其他泰门债主的仆人相遇)

凡罗家仆人甲　咱们碰见得很巧;早安,泰特斯,霍坦歇斯。

TITUS	The like to you, kind Varro.
HORTENSIUS	Lucius, what, do we meet together?
LUCIUS' SERVANT	Ay, and I think one business does command us all,
	For mine is money.
TITUS	So is theirs and ours.

[*Enter Philotus.*]

LUCIUS' SERVANT	And Sir Philotus too!
PHILOTUS	Good day at once.
LUCIUS' SERVANT	Welcome, good brother.
	What do you think the hour?
PHILOTUS	Labouring for nine.
LUCIUS' SERVANT	So much?
PHILOTUS	Is not my lord seen yet?
LUCIUS' SERVANT	Not yet.
PHILOTUS	I wonder on't: he was wont to shine at seven.
LUCIUS' SERVANT	Ay, but the days are waxed shorter with him:
	You must consider that a prodigal course
	Is like the sun's,
	But not, like his, recoverable. I fear
	'Tis deepest winter in Lord Timon's purse: that is,
	One may reach deep enough, and yet find little.
PHILOTUS	I am of your fear for that.
TITUS	I'll show you how t'observe a strange event.
	Your lord sends now for money?
HORTENSIUS	Most true, he does.
TITUS	And he wears jewels now of Timon's gift,
	For which I wait for money.
HORTENSIUS	It is against my heart.

泰　特　斯　　早安，凡罗家的大哥。

霍坦歇斯　　路歇斯家的大哥！怎么！你也来了吗？

路歇斯家仆人　是的，我想我们都是为着同一的目的来的；我为讨钱而来。

泰　特　斯　　他们和我们都是来讨钱的。

（菲洛特斯上）

路歇斯家仆人　菲洛特斯也来了！

菲洛特斯　　各位早安。

路歇斯家仆人　欢迎，好兄弟。你想现在是什么时候了？

菲洛特斯　　快九点钟啦。

路歇斯家仆人　这么晚了吗？

菲洛特斯　　还没有看见泰门大爷吗？

路歇斯家仆人　还没有。

菲洛特斯　　那可怪了；他平常总是七点钟就起来的。

路歇斯家仆人　嗯，可是他的白昼现在已经比从前短了；你该知道一个浪子所走的路程是跟太阳一般的，可是他并不像太阳一样周而复始。我怕在泰门大爷的钱囊里，已经是岁晚寒深的暮冬时候了，你尽管一直把手伸到底里，恐怕还是一无所得。

菲洛特斯　　我也担着这样的心。

泰　特　斯　　我可以提醒你一件奇怪的事情。你家大爷现在差你来要钱。

霍坦歇斯　　一点不错，他差我来要钱。

泰　特　斯　　可是他身上还戴着泰门送给他的珠宝，我就是到这儿来等他把这珠宝的钱还我的。

霍坦歇斯　　我虽然奉命而来，心里可是老大不愿。

LUCIUS' SERVANT	Mark how strange it shows:
	Timon in this should pay more than he owes,
	And e'en as if your lord should wear rich jewels,
	And send for money for 'em.
HORTENSIUS	I'm weary of this charge, the gods can witness:
	I know my lord hath spent of Timon's wealth,
	And now ingratitude makes it worse than stealth.
VARRO'S FIRST SERVANT	Yes, mine's three thousand crowns; what's yours?
LUCIUS' SERVANT	Five thousand mine.
VARRO'S FIRST SERVANT	'Tis much deep, and it should seem by th' sum,
	Your master's confidence was above mine,
	Else surely his had equalled.
	[*Enter Flaminius.*]
TITUS	One of Lord Timon's men.
LUCIUS' SERVANT	Flaminius! Sir, a word: pray, is my lord ready to come forth?
FLAMINIUS	No, indeed, he is not.
TITUS	We attend his lordship: pray signify so much.
FLAMINIUS	I need not tell him that: he knows you are too diligent.
	[*Exit.*]
	[*Enter Steward Flavius in a cloak, muffled.*]
LUCIUS' SERVANT	Ha? Is not that his steward muffled so?
	He goes away in a cloud. Call him, call him.
TITUS	Do you hear, sir?
VARRO'S SECOND SERVANT	By your leave, sir —
FLAVIUS	What do you ask of me, my friend?
TITUS	We wait for certain money here, sir.

路歇斯家仆人	你瞧，事情多么奇怪，泰门应该还人家的钱比他实在欠下的债还多；好像你家主人佩戴了他的珍贵的珠宝以后，还应该向他讨还珠宝的价钱一样。
霍坦歇斯	我真不愿意干这种差使。我知道我家主人挥霍了泰门的财产，现在还要干这样忘恩负义的事，真是窃贼不如了。
凡罗家仆人甲	是的，我要向他讨还三千克朗，你呢？
路歇斯家仆人	我的是五千克朗。
凡罗家仆人甲	还是你比我多；照这数目看起来，你家主人对他的交情比我家主人深得多了，否则不会有这样的差别的。

（弗莱米涅斯上）

泰特斯	他是泰门大爷的一个仆人。
路歇斯家仆人	弗莱米涅斯！大哥，说句话。请问大爷就要出来了吗？
弗莱米涅斯	不，他还不想出来呢。
泰特斯	我们都在等着他；请你去向他通报一声。
弗莱米涅斯	我不必通报他；他知道你们是经常上门的。（弗莱米涅斯下）

（弗莱维斯穿外套蒙首上）

路歇斯家仆人	嘿！那个蒙住了脸的，不是他的管家吗？他躲躲闪闪地去了；叫住他，叫住他。
泰特斯	你听见吗，总管？
凡罗家仆人乙	对不起，总管。
弗莱维斯	你有什么事要问我，朋友？
泰特斯	我们在这儿等着要拿回几个钱，总管。

FLAVIUS	Ay,
	If money were as certain as your waiting,
	'Twere sure enough.
	Why then prefferred you not your sums and bills
	When your false masters eat of my lord's meat?
	Then they could smile and fawn upon his debts
	And take down th'interest into their glutt'nous maws.
	You do yourselves but wrong to stir me up:
	Let me pass quietly.
	Believe't, my lord and I have made an end:
	I have no more to reckon, he to spend.
LUCIUS' SERVANT	Ay, but this answer will not serve.
FLAVIUS	If 'twill not serve, 'tis not so base as you,
	For you serve knaves. [*Exit.*]
VARRO'S FIRST SERVANT	How? What does his cashiered worship mutter?
VARRO'S SECOND SERVANT	No matter what: he's poor, and that's revenge enough.
	Who can speak broader than he that has no house to
	put his head in? Such may rail against great buildings.
	[*Enter Servilius.*]
TITUS	O, here's Servilius: now we shall know some answer.
SERVILIUS	If I might beseech you, gentlemen, to repair some
	other hour, I should derive much from't, for, take't
	of my soul, my lord leans wondrously to discontent:
	hiscomfortable temper has forsook him; he's much out
	of health, and keeps his chamber.
LUCIUS' SERVANT	Many do keep their chambers are not sick,
	And if it be so far beyond his health,

弗莱维斯	哼,当你们那些黑心的主人们吃着我家大爷的肉食的时候,为什么你们不把债票送上来要钱?那个时候他们是不把他的欠款放在心上的,只知道忙着胁肩谄笑,把利息吞下他们贪馋的胃里。你们跟我吵有什么用呢?让我安安静静地过去吧。相信我,我家大爷跟我已经解除了主仆的名分;我没有账可管,他也没有钱可用了。
路歇斯家仆人	我们可不能拿你这样的话回去交代啊。
弗莱维斯	我的话倒是老实话,不像你们的主人都是些无耻小人。

(下)

凡罗家仆人甲	怎么!这位卸了职的老爷子咕噜些什么?
凡罗家仆人乙	随他咕噜些什么;他是个苦老头儿,理他作甚?连一间可以钻进头去的屋子也没有的人,见了高楼大厦当然会痛骂的。

(塞维律斯上)

泰 特 斯	啊!塞维律斯来了,现在我们可以得到一些答复了。
塞维律斯	各位朋友,要是你们愿意改日再来,我就感谢不尽了;不瞒列位说,我家大爷今天心境很不好;他身子也有点不大舒服,不能起来。
路歇斯家仆人	有许多人睡在床上不起来,并不是为了害病的缘故。

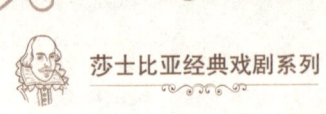

	Methinks he should the sooner pay his debts
	And make a clear way to the gods.
SERVILIUS	Good gods!
TITUS	We cannot take this for answer, sir.
FLAMINIUS	[*Within.*] Servilius, help! My lord, my lord!
	[*Enter Timon, in a rage.*]
TIMON	What, are my doors opposed against my passage?
	Have I been ever free, and must my house
	Be my retentive enemy, my jail?
	The place which I have feasted, does it now,
	Like all mankind, show me an iron heart?
LUCIUS' SERVANT	Put in now, Titus.
TITUS	My lord, here is my bill.
LUCIUS' SERVANT	Here's mine.
HORTENSIUS	And mine, my lord.
VARRO'S FIRST AND SECOND SERVANTS	And ours, my lord.
PHILOTUS	All our bills.
TIMON	Knock me down with 'em: cleave me to the girdle.
LUCIUS' SERVANT	Alas, my lord.
TIMON	Cut my heart in sums.
TITUS	Mine, fifty talents.
TIMON	Tell out my blood.
LUCIUS' SERVANT	Five thousand crowns, my lord.
TIMON	Five thousand drops pays that. What yours? And yours?
VARRO'S FIRST SERVANT	My lord —
VARRO'S SECOND SERVANT	My lord —

	要是他真的有病，我想他更应该早一点把债还清，这才可以撒手归天。
塞维律斯	天哪！
泰 特 斯	我们不能拿这样的话回去交代哩。
弗莱米涅斯	（在内）塞维律斯，赶快！大爷！大爷！
	（泰门暴怒上，弗莱米涅斯随上）
泰　　门	什么！我自己的门都不许我通过吗？我从来不曾受别人管过，现在我自己的屋子却变成了拘禁我的敌人、我的监狱吗？我曾经举行过宴会的地方，难道也像所有的人类一样，用一颗铁石的心肠对待我吗？
路歇斯家仆人	跟他说去，泰特斯。
泰 特 斯	大爷，这儿是我的债票。
路歇斯家仆人	这儿是我的。
霍坦歇斯	还有我的，大爷。
凡罗家仆人甲 凡罗家仆人乙	还有我们的，大爷。
菲洛特斯	我们的债票都在这儿。
泰　　门	用你们的债票把我打倒，把我腰斩了吧。
路歇斯家仆人	唉！大爷——
泰　　门	剖开我的心来。
泰 特 斯	我的账上是五十个泰伦。
泰　　门	把我的血一滴一滴地数出来。
路歇斯家仆人	五千个克朗，大爷。
泰　　门	还你五千滴血。你要多少？你呢？
凡罗家仆人甲	大爷——
凡罗家仆人乙	大爷——

TIMON	Tear me, take me, and the gods fall upon you! [*Exit Timon.*]
HORTENSIUS	'Faith, I perceive our masters may throw their caps at their money: these debts may well be called desperate ones, for a madman owes 'em. [*Exeunt.*]

SCENE V The Same. A Hall in Timon's House continues.

[*Enter Timon and Flavius.*]

TIMON	They have e'en put my breath from me, the slaves. Creditors? Devils!
FLAVIUS	My dear lord —
TIMON	What if it should be so?
FLAVIUS	My lord —
TIMON	I'll have it so. My steward!
FLAVIUS	Here, my lord.
TIMON	So fitly? Go, bid all my friends again, Lucius, Lucullus, and Sempronius — all luxurs, all. I'll once more feast the rascals.
FLAVIUS	O my lord, You only speak from your distracted soul; There is not so much left to furnish out A moderate table.
TIMON	Be it not in thy care: go, I charge thee, invite them all. Let in the tide Of knaves once more: my cook and I'll provide. [*Exeunt.*]

泰　　　门　扯碎我的四肢，把我的身体拿了去吧；天神的愤怒降在你们身上！（下）

霍坦歇斯　我看我们的主人的债是讨不回来的了，因为欠债的是个疯子。（同下）

第五场　同前。

（泰门及弗莱维斯重上）

泰　　　门　他们简直不容我有一点儿喘息的工夫，这些奴才们！什么债主，简直是魔鬼！

弗莱维斯　我的好大爷——

泰　　　门　要是果然这样呢？

弗莱维斯　大爷——

泰　　　门　我一定这么办。管家！

弗莱维斯　有，大爷。

泰　　　门　很好！去，再把我的朋友们一起请来，路歇斯，路库勒斯，辛普洛涅斯，叫他们大家都来；我还要宴请一次这些恶人。

弗莱维斯　啊，大爷！您这些话只是一时气愤之言；别说请客，现在就是略为备一些酒食的钱也没有了。

泰　　　门　你别管，去吧。我叫你把他们全都请来，让那些混账东西再进一次我的门，我的厨子跟我会预备好东西给他们吃的。（同下）

SCENE VI *The Senate House.*

[*Enter three Senators at one door, Alcibiades meeting them, with Attendants.*]

FIRST SENATOR My lord, you have my voice to it. The fault's
Bloody: 'tis necessary he should die.
Nothing emboldens sin so much as mercy.

SECOND SENATOR Most true; the law shall bruise 'em.

[*Enter Alcibiades, attended.*]

ALCIBIADES [*Comes forward.*] Honour, health, and compassion to the senate!

FIRST SENATOR Now, captain.

ALCIBIADES I am an humble suitor to your virtues;
For pity is the virtue of the law,
And none but tyrants use it cruelly.
It pleases time and fortune to lie heavy
Upon a friend of mine, who in hot blood
Hath stepped into the law ,which is past depth
To those that, without heed, do plunge into't.
He is a man, setting his fate aside,
Of comely virtues:
Nor did he soil the fact with cowardice —
And honour in him which buys out his fault —
But with a noble fury and fair spirit,
Seeing his reputation touched to death,
He did oppose his foe,
And with such sober and unnoted passion
He did behave his anger, ere 'was spent,

第六场　同前。元老院

（众元老列坐议事）

元老甲　大人，您的意见我很赞同，这是一件重大的过失，他必须判处死刑；姑息的结果只是放纵了罪恶。

元老乙　一点不错；法律必须给他一些惩罚。

（艾西巴第斯率侍从上）

艾西巴第斯　（上前）愿荣耀、康健和仁慈归于各位元老！

元老甲　请了，将军。

艾西巴第斯　我是你们的一个卑微的请愿者。人家说，法律不外人情，只有暴君酷吏才会借着法律的威严肆其荼毒。我的一个朋友因为一时之愤，无意中陷入法网。虽然他现在遭逢不幸，可是他也是很有品行的人，并不是卑怯无耻之流，单这一点也就可以补赎他的过失了；他因为眼看他的名誉受到致命的污辱，所以才挺身而起，光明正大地和他的敌人决斗；就是当他们兵刃相交的时候，他也始终不动声色，就像不过跟人家辩论一场

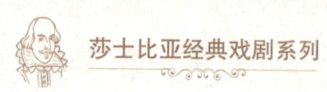

莎士比亚经典戏剧系列

      As if he had but proved an argument.
FIRST SENATOR You undergo too strict a paradox,
      Striving to make an ugly deed look fair:
      Your words have took such pains as if they laboured
      To bring manslaughter into form and set quarrelling
      Upon the head of valour; which indeed
      Is valour misbegot, and came into the world
      When sects and factions were newly born.
      He's truly valiant that can wisely suffer
      The worst that man can breathe,
      And make his wrongs his outsides,
      To wear them like his raiment, carelessly,
      And ne'er prefer his injuries to his heart
      To bring it into danger.
      If wrongs be evils and enforce us kill,
      What folly 'tis to hazard life for ill!
ALCIBIADES My lord —
FIRST SENATOR You cannot make gross sins look clear:
      To revenge is no valour, but to bear.
ALCIBIADES My lords, then, under favour, pardon me
      If I speak like a captain.
      Why do fond men expose themselves to battle,
      And not endure all threats? Sleep upon't,
      And let the foes quietly cut their throats
      Without repugnancy? If there be
      Such valour in the bearing, what make we
      Abroad? Why then, women are more valiant
      That stay at home, if bearing carry it.

是非一样。

元老甲　您想把一件恶事说得像一件好事，恐怕难以自圆其说；您的话全然是饰词强辩，有心替杀人犯辩护，把斗殴当作勇敢，可惜这种勇敢却是误用了的。真正勇敢的人，应当能够智慧地忍受最难堪的屈辱，不以身外的荣辱介怀，用息事宁人的态度避免无谓的横祸。要是屈辱可以使我们杀人，那么为了气愤而冒着生命的危险，是一件多么愚蠢的事！

艾西巴第斯　大人——

元老甲　您不能使重大的罪恶化为清白；报复不是勇敢，忍受才是勇敢。

艾西巴第斯　各位大人，我是一个武人，请你们恕我说句武人的话。为什么愚蠢的人们宁愿在战场上捐躯，不知道忍受各种的威胁呢？为什么他们不高枕而眠，让敌人从容割破他们的咽喉而不加抗拒呢？要是忍受果然是这样勇敢的行为，那么我们为什么要去远征国外呢？照这样说来，那么在家内安居的妇人女子才是更勇敢的，驴子也要比狮子英雄得多了；要是忍受是一种智慧，那

>   And the ass more captain than the lion, the fellow
>   Loaden with irons wiser than the judge,
>   If wisdom be in suffering. O my lords,
>   As you are great, be pitifully good.
>   Who cannot condemn rashness in cold blood?
>   To kill, I grant, is sin's extremest gust,
>   But in defence, by mercy, 'tis most just.
>   To be in anger is impiety,
>   But who is man that is not angry?
>   Weigh but the crime with this.
> SECOND SENATOR   You breathe in vain.
> ALCIBIADES   In vain? His service done
>   At Lacedaemon and Byzantium
>   Were a sufficient briber for his life.
> FIRST SENATOR   What's that?
> ALCIBIADES   Why, I say, my lords, he's done fair service,
>   And slain in fight many of your enemies:
>   How full of valour did he bear himself
>   In the last conflict, and made plenteous wounds!
> SECOND SENATOR   He has made too much plenty with 'em.
>   He's a sworn rioter: he has a sin
>   That often drowns him, and takes his valour prisoner:
>   If there were no foes, that were enough
>   To overcome him. In that beastly fury
>   He has been known to commit outrages
>   And cherish factions: 'tis inferred to us,
>   His days are foul and his drink dangerous.
> FIRST SENATOR   He dies.

么铁索锒铛的囚犯,也比法官更聪明了。啊,各位大人!你们身膺众望,应该仁爱为怀。谁不知道残酷的暴行是罪不容赦的?杀人者处极刑,可是为了自卫而杀人,却是正当的行为。负气使性,虽然为正人君子所不齿,然而人非木石,谁没有一时的气愤呢?你们在判定他的罪名以前,请先斟酌人情,不要矫枉过正才好。

元老乙　您这些话全是白说。

艾西巴第斯　白说!他在斯巴达和拜占庭两次战役中所立的功劳,难道不能赎回他的一死吗?

元老甲　那是怎么一回事?

艾西巴第斯　我说,各位大人,他曾经立下不少的功劳,在战争中杀死你们的许多敌人。在上次作战的时候,他是多么勇敢,手刃了多少人!

元老乙　他杀过太多的人,他是个好乱成性的家伙;要是没有人跟他作对,他也要找人家吵闹,因为他有这样的坏脾气,也不知闹过多少回事、引起多少回的纷争了;我们久已风闻他的酗酒寻衅、行为不检的劣迹。

元老甲　他必须处死。

ALCIBIADES	Hard fate! He might have died in war.
	My lords, if not for any parts in him —
	Though his right arm might purchase his own time
	And be in debt to none — yet, more to move you,
	Take my deserts to his and join 'em both.
	And for I know
	Your reverend ages love security,
	I'll pawn my victories, all my honour to you,
	Upon his good returns.
	If by this crime he owes the law his life,
	Why, let the war receive't in valiant gore;
	For law is strict, and war is nothing more.
FIRST SENATOR	We are for law: he dies: urge it no more
	On height of our displeasure. Friend, or brother,
	He forfeits his own blood that spills another.
ALCIBIADES	Must it be so? It must not be.
	My lords, I do beseech you know me.
SECOND SENATOR	How?
ALCIBIADES	Call me to your remembrances.
THIRD SENATOR	What?
ALCIBIADES	I cannot think but your age has forgot me:
	It could not else be, I should prove so base
	To sue and be denied such common grace.
	My wounds ache at you.
FIRST SENATOR	Do you dare our anger?
	'Tis in few words, but spacious in effect:
	We banish thee for ever.
ALCIBIADES	Banish me?
	Banish your dotage, banish usury

| 艾西巴第斯 | 残酷的命运！早知如此，他就该死在战场上。各位大人，要是他的功绩才能不能替他自己赎罪，那么我可以拿我自己的微劳一并作为抵押，请你们宽恕了他的死罪；我知道你们这样年高的人都喜欢有一个确实的保证，所以我愿意把我历次的胜利和我的荣誉向你们担保，他一定不会有负你们的矜宥。要是他这次所犯的罪，按照法律必须用生命抵偿，那么让他洒血沙场，英勇而死吧；因为战争是和法律同样无情的。 |

| 元老甲 | 我们只知道秉公执法，他必须死。不要再絮渎了，免得惹起我们的恼怒。即使他是我们的朋友或是兄弟，杀了人也必须抵命。 |

| 艾西巴第斯 | 一定要这样办吗？不，一定不能这样办。各位大人，我请求你们，想一想我是什么人。 |

| 元老甲 | 怎么！ |

| 艾西巴第斯 | 请你们想一想我是什么人。 |

| 元老丙 | 什么！ |

| 艾西巴第斯 | 我想你们一定年老健忘，想不起我了；否则我这样向你们卑辞请求这么一点小小的恩惠，总不至于会被你们拒绝的。我身上的伤痕在为你们而疼痛哩。 |

| 元老甲 | 你胆敢惹我们生气吗？好，听着，我们没有很多的话说，可是我们的话是言出如山的：我们宣布把你永远放逐。 |

| 艾西巴第斯 | 把我放逐！把你们自己的糊涂放逐了吧；把你们放债 |

	That makes the senate ugly.
FIRST SENATOR	If after two days' shine Athens contain thee,
	Attend our weightier judgment. And, not to swell our spirit,
	He shall be executed presently. [*Exeunt Senators.*]
ALCIBIADES	Now the gods keep you old enough that you may live
	Only in bone, that none may look on you!
	I'm worse than mad: I have kept back their foes
	While they have told their money and let out
	Their coin upon large interest, I myself
	Rich only in large hurts. All those for this?
	Is this the balsam that the usuring senate
	Pours into captains' wounds? Banishment!
	It comes not ill: I hate not to be banished.
	It is a cause worthy my spleen and fury,
	That I may strike at Athens. I'll cheer up
	My discontented troops, and lay for hearts.
	'Tis honour with most lands to be at odds.
	Soldiers should brook as little wrongs as gods. [*Exit.*]

SCENE VII *A Banqueting Hall in Timon's House.*

[*Enter divers friends, Lords and Senators, at several doors.*]

FIRST LORD	The good time of day to you, sir.
SECOND LORD	I also wish it to you. I think this honourable lord did

营私、秽迹昭彰的腐化行为放逐了吧！

元老甲　要是在两天以后，你仍旧逗留在雅典境内，我们就要判处你加倍的重罪。至于你那位朋友，为了让我们耳目中清静一些起见，我们就要把他立刻处决。（众元老同下）

艾西巴第斯　愿神明保佑你们长寿，让你们枯瘦得只剩一副骨头，谁也不来瞧你们一眼！真把我气疯了；我替他们打退了敌人，让他们安安稳稳地在一边数他们的钱，用高利息放债，我自己却只得到了满身的伤痕：这一切不过换到了今天这样的结果吗？难道这就是那放高利贷的元老院替将士伤口敷上的油膏吗？放逐！那倒不是坏事；我不恨他们把我放逐；我可以借着这个理由，举兵攻击雅典，向他们发泄我的愤怒。我要去鼓动我的愤愤不平的部队；军人们像天神一样，是不能忍受丝毫的侮辱的。（下）

第七场　同前。泰门家中的宴会厅

（音乐；室内排列餐桌，众仆立侍；若干贵族、元老及余人等自各门分别上）

贵族甲　早安，大人。
贵族乙　早安。我想这位可尊敬的贵人前天不过是把我们试探

	but try us this other day.
FIRST LORD	Upon that were my thoughts tiring when we encountered. I hope it is not so low with him as he made it seem in the trial of his several friends.
SECOND LORD	It should not be, by the persuasion of his new feasting.
FIRST LORD	I should think so: he hath sent me an earnest inviting, which many my near occasions did urge me to put off, but he hath conjured me beyond them, and I must needs appear.
SECOND LORD	In like manner was I in debt to my importunate business, but he would not hear my excuse. I am sorry when he sent to borrow of me that my provision was out.
FIRST LORD	I am sick of that grief too, as I understand how all things go.
SECOND LORD	Every man here's so. What would he have borrowed of you?
FIRST LORD	A thousand pieces.
SECOND LORD	A thousand pieces?
FIRST LORD	What of you?
SECOND LORD	He sent to me, sir — here he comes.

[*Enter Timon and Attendants.*]

TIMON	With all my heart, gentlemen both; and how fare you?
FIRST LORD	Ever at the best, hearing well of your lordship.
SECOND LORD	The swallow follows not summer more willing than we your lordship.
TIMON	[*Aside.*] Nor more willingly leaves winter, such summer birds are men. — Gentlemen, our dinner will not recompense this long stay. Feast your ears with the

贵　族　甲		我刚才也这么想着,我希望他并不真的穷到像他故意装给朋友们看的那个样子。
贵　族　乙		照他这次重开盛宴的情形看来,他并没有真穷。
贵　族　甲		我也这样想。他很诚恳地邀请我,我本来还有许多事情,实在抽不出身,可是因为他的盛情难却,所以不能不拨冗而来。
贵　族　乙		我也有许多要事在身,可是他一定不肯放过我。我很抱歉,当他叫人来问我借钱的时候,我刚巧手边没有现款。
贵　族　甲		我知道了他这种情形之后,心里也难过得很。
贵　族　乙		这儿每一个人都有这样的感觉。他要向您借多少钱?
贵　族　甲		一千块。
贵　族　乙		一千块!
贵　族　甲		您呢?
贵　族　丙		他叫人到我那儿去,大人,——他来了。

（泰门及侍从等上）

泰　　　门		竭诚欢迎,两位老兄;你们都好吗?
贵　族　甲		托您的福,大人。
贵　族　乙		燕子跟随夏天,也不及我们跟随您这样踊跃。
泰　　　门		(旁白)你们离开我也比燕子离开冬天还快;人就是这种趋炎避冷的鸟儿。——各位朋友,今天肴馔不周,

	music awhile, if they will fare so harshly o'th trumpet's sound: we shall to't presently.
FIRST LORD	I hope it remains not unkindly with your lordship that I returned you an empty messenger.
TIMON	O, sir, let it not trouble you.
SECOND LORD	My noble lord —
TIMON	Ah, my good friend, what cheer?

[*The banquet brought in.*]

SECOND LORD	My most honourable lord, I am e'en sick of shame, that, when your lordship this other day sent to me, I was so unfortunate a beggar.
TIMON	Think not on't, sir.
SECOND LORD	If you had sent but two hours before, —
TIMON	Let it not cumber your better remembrance. — [*To Servants, who bring in coverd dishes.*] Come, bring in all together.
SECOND LORD	All covered dishes!
FIRST LORD	Royal cheer, I warrant you.
THIRD LORD	Doubt not that, if money and the season can yield it.
FIRST LORD	How do you? What's the news?
THIRD LORD	Alcibiades is banished: hear you of it?
FIRST LORD / SECOND LORD	Alcibiades banished?
THIRD LORD	'Tis so, be sure of it.
FIRST LORD	How? How?
SECOND LORD	I pray you upon what?
TIMON	My worthy friends, will you draw near?
THIRD LORD	I'll tell you more anon. Here's a noble feast toward.
SECOND LORD	This is the old man still.

又累你们久等,实在抱歉万分;要是你们不嫌喇叭的声音刺耳,请先饱听一下音乐,我们就可以入席了。

贵族甲　前天累尊价空劳往返,希望您不要见怪。

泰　门　啊!老兄,那是小事,请您不必放在心上。

贵族乙　大人——

泰　门　啊!我的好朋友,什么事?

（筵席摆上台）

贵族乙　大人,我真是说不出的惭愧,前天您叫人来看我的时候,不巧我正是身无分文。

泰　门　老兄不必介意。

贵族乙　要是您再早两点钟叫人来——

泰　门　请您不要把这种事留在记忆里。（众仆端酒食上）来,把所有的盘子放在一起。

贵族乙　盘子上全都罩着盖!

贵族甲　一定是奇珍异味哩。

贵族丙　那还用说吗,只要是出了钱买得到的东西。

贵族甲　您好?近来有什么消息?

贵族丙　艾西巴第斯被放逐了;您听见人家说起没有?

贵族甲
贵族乙 } 艾西巴第斯被放逐了!

贵族丙　是的,这消息是的确的。

贵族甲　怎么?怎么?

贵族乙　请问是为了什么原因?

泰　门　各位好朋友,大家过来吧。

贵族丙　等会儿我再详细告诉您。看来又是一场盛大的欢宴。

贵族乙　他还是原来那样子。

THIRD LORD Will't hold? Will't hold?
SECOND LORD It does: but time will — and so —
THIRD LORD I do conceive.
TIMON Each man to his stool with that spur as he would to the lip of his mistress: your diet shall be in all places alike. Make not a city feast of it, to let the meat cool ere we can agree upon the first place. Sit, sit. [*They sit.*] The gods require our thanks. — You great benefactors, sprinkle our society with thankfulness. For your own gifts, make yourselves praised: but reserve still to give, lest your deities be despised. Lend to each man enough that one need not lend to another, for were your godheads to borrow of men, men would forsake the gods. Make the meat be beloved more than the man that gives it. Let no assembly of twenty be without a score of villains: if there sit twelve women at the table, let a dozen of them be as they are. The rest of your foes, O gods — the senators of Athens, together with the common tag of people — what is amiss in them, you gods, make suitable for destruction. For these my present friends, as they are to me nothing, so in nothing bless them, and to nothing are they welcome.— Uncover, dogs, and lap!

[*The dishes are uncovered and seen to be full of warmwater and stones.*]

SOME LORDS What does his lordship mean?
OTHER LORDS I know not.
TIMON May you a better feast never behold,
You knot of mouth-friends. Smoke and lukewarm water

贵族丙	这样子能够维持长久吗？
贵族乙	也许，可是——那就——
贵族丙	我明白您的意思。
泰　门	请大家用着和爱人接吻那样热烈的情绪，各人就各人的座位吧；你们的菜肴是完全一律的。不要拘泥礼节，逊让得把肉菜都冷了。请坐，请坐。（众人坐下）我们必须先向神明道谢：——

神啊，我们感谢你们的施与，赞颂你们的恩惠；可是不要把你们所有的一切完全给人，免得你们神灵也要被人蔑视。借足够的钱给每一个人，不使他再转借给别人；因为如果你们神灵也要向人类告贷，人类是会把神明舍弃的。让人们重视肉食，甚于把肉食赏给他们的人。让每一处有二十个男子的所在，聚集着二十个恶徒；要是有十二个妇人围桌而坐，让她们中间的十二个人保持她们的本色。神啊！那些雅典的元老们，以及黎民众庶，请你们鉴察他们的罪恶，让他们遭受毁灭的命运吧。至于我这些在座的朋友，他们本来对于我漠不相关，所以我不给他们任何的祝福，我所用来款待他们的也只有空虚的无物。揭开来，狗子们，舔你们的盆子吧。（众盘揭开，内满贮温水和石头）

一宾客	他这种举动是什么意思？
另一宾客	我不知道。
泰　门	请你们永远不再见到比这更好的宴会，你们这一群口头的朋友！蒸汽和温水是你们最好的饮食。这是泰门

Is your perfection. This is Timon's last,
Who, stuck and spangled with your flatteries,
Washes it off, and sprinkles in your faces
   [*Throws water at them.*] Your reeking villainy. Live loathed and long,
Most smiling, smooth, detested parasites,
Courteous destroyers, affable wolves, meek bears,
You fools of fortune, trencher-friends, time's flies,
Cap and knee slaves, vapours, and minute-jacks!
Of man and beast the infinite malady
Crust you quite o'er! —
   [*A Lord gets up to leave.*]
What, dost thou go?
Soft, take thy physic firs. — Thou too, and thou.
   [*Throws the stones at them.*]
Stay, I will lend thee money, borrow none.
   [*Exeunt the Lords, Leaving their caps and gowns.*]
What, all in motion? Henceforth be no feast,
Whereat a villain's not a welcome guest.
Burn, house! Sink, Athens! Henceforth hated be
Of Timon, man and all humanity! [*Exit.*]
   [*Enter the Senators with other Lords.*]

FIRST LORD How now, my lords?
SECOND LORD Know you the quality of Lord Timon's fury?
THIRD LORD Push! Did you see my cap?
FOURTH LORD I have lost my gown.
FIRST LORD He's but a mad lord, and nought but humourous sways him. He gave me a jewel th'other day, and now he has

最后一次的宴会了；他因为被你们的谄媚迷住了心窍，所以要把它洗干净，把你们这些恶臭的奸诈仍旧洒还给你们。（浇水于众客脸上）愿你们老而不死，永远受人憎恶，你们这些微笑的、柔和的、可厌的寄生虫，彬彬有礼的破坏者。驯良的豺狼，温顺的熊，命运的弄人，酒食征逐的朋友，趋炎附势的青蝇，脱帽屈膝的奴才，水汽一样轻浮的幺麽小丑！一切人畜的恶症侵蚀你们的全身！（一贵族起身欲走）什么！你要走了吗？且慢！你还没有把你的教训带去，——还有你，——还有你；（向众贵族扔石块）等一等，我有钱借给你们哩，我不要向你们借钱呀！（将盘子掷众客身，众下）什么！大家都要走了吗？从此以后，让每一个宴会上把奸人尊为上客吧。屋子，烧起来呀！雅典，陆沉了吧！从此以后，泰门将要痛恨一切的人类了！（下）

（众贵族、元老等重上）

贵　族　甲	哎哟，各位大人！
贵　族　乙	您知道泰门发怒的缘故吗？
贵　族　丙	嘿！您看见我的帽子吗？
贵　族　丁	我的袍子也丢了。
贵　族　甲	他已经发了疯啦，完全在逗着他的性子乱闹。前天他给我一颗宝石，现在他又把它从我的帽子上打下来了。

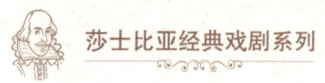

                        beat it out of my hat. Did you see my jewel? [*They search.*]

THIRD LORD   Did you see my cap?

SECOND LORD   Here 'tis.

FOURTH LORD   Here lies my gown.

FIRST LORD   Let's make no stay.

SECOND LORD   Lord Timon's mad.

THIRD LORD   I feel't upon my bones.

FOURTH LORD   One day he gives us diamonds, next day stones.

        [*Exeunt the Senators, and Lords.*]

你们看见我的宝石吗？（众贵族搜寻）

贵　族　丙　您看见我的帽子吗？

贵　族　乙　在这儿。

贵　族　丁　这儿是我的袍子。

贵　族　甲　我们还是快走吧。

贵　族　乙　泰门已经疯了。

贵　族　丙　他把我的骨头都捶痛了呢。

贵　族　丁　他高兴就给我们金刚钻，不高兴就用石子扔我们。

（同下）

Act IV

SCENE I *Without the Walls of Athens.*

[*Enter Timon.*]

TIMON Let me look back upon thee. O thou wall
That girdles in those wolves, dive in the earth,
And fence not Athens! Matrons, turn incontinent,
Obedience fail in children! Slaves and fools,
Pluck the grave wrinkled senate from the bench,
And minister in their steads! To general filths
Convert o'th'instant, green virginity:
Do't in your parents' eyes! Bankrupts, hold fast
Rather than render back; out with your knives,
And cut your trusters' throats! Bound servants, steal!
Large-handed robbers your grave masters are,
And pill by law. Maid, to thy master's bed,
Thy mistress is o'th' brothel! Son of sixteen,
Pluck the lined crutch from thy old limping sire,
With it beat out his brains! Piety and fear,
Religion to the gods, peace, justice, truth,
Domestic awe, night-rest, and neighbourhood,
Instruction, manners, mysteries and trades,
Degrees, observances, customs and laws,
Decline to your confounding contraries,
And yet confusion live! Plagues incident to men,
Your potent and infectious fevers heap

第四幕

第一场 雅典城外

（泰门上）

泰　门　让我回头瞧瞧你。城啊，你包藏着如许的豺狼，快快陆沉吧，不要再替雅典做藩篱！已婚的妇人们，淫荡起来吧！子女们不要听父母的话！奴才们和傻瓜们，把那些年高德劭的元老们拉下来，你们自己坐上他们的位置吧！娇嫩的处女变成人尽可夫的娼妓，当着你们父母的眼前跟别人通奸吧！破产的人，不要偿还你们的欠款，用刀子割破你们债主的咽喉吧！仆人们，放手偷窃吧！你们庄严的主人都是借着法律的名义杀人越货的大盗。婢女们，睡到你们主人的床上去吧，你们的主妇已经做卖淫妇去了！十六岁的儿子，夺下你步履龙钟的老父手里的拐杖，把他的脑浆敲出来吧！孝亲敬神的美德、和平公义的正道、齐家睦邻的要义、教育、礼仪、百工的技巧、尊卑的品秩、风俗、习惯，一起陷于混乱吧！加害于人身的各种瘟疫，向雅典伸展你们的毒手，播散你们猖獗传染的热病！让风湿钻进我们那些元老的骨髓，使他们手脚瘫痪！让淫欲放荡占领我们那些少年人的心，使他们反抗道德，沉溺在狂乱之中！每一个雅典人身上播下了疥癣疮毒的种子，让他们一个个害起癞病！让他们的呼吸中都含着毒素，谁和他们来往做朋友都会中毒而死！（将衣服

On Athens, ripe for stroke! Thou cold sciatica,
Cripple our senators that their limbs may halt
As lamely as their manners. Lust and liberty
Creep in the minds and marrows of our youth,
That gainst the stream of virtue they may strive
And drown themselves in riot! Itches, blains,
Sow all th'Athenian bosoms, and their crop
Be general leprosy! Breath infect breath,
That their society, as their friendship, may
Be merely poison! Nothing I'll bear from thee
［*Tears off his clothes.*］But nakedness, thou detestable town.
Take thou that too, with multiplying bans!
Timon will to the woods, where he shall find
Th'unkindest beast more kinder than mankind.
The gods confound — hear me, you good gods all —
Th'Athenians both within and out that wall,
And grant, as Timon grows, his hate may grow
To the whole race of mankind, high and low! Amen.
［*Exit.*］

SCENE II *Athens. A Room in Timon's House.*

［*Enter Steward Flavius with two or three Servants.*］

FIRST SERVANT Hear you, master steward, where's our master?
Are we undone, cast off, nothing remaining?

FLAVIUS Alack, my fellows, what should I say to you?
Let me be recorded by the righteous gods,

扯下)除了我这赤裸裸的一身以外,我什么也不带走,你这可憎的城市!我给你的只有无穷的诅咒!泰门要到树林里去,和最凶恶的野兽做伴侣,比起无情的人类来,它们是要善良得多了。天上一切神明,听着我,把那城墙内外的雅典人一起毁灭了吧!求你们让泰门把他的仇恨扩展到全体人类,不分贵贱高低!阿门。(下)

第二场 雅典。泰门家中一室

(弗莱维斯及二、三仆人上)

仆甲 请问总管,我们的主人呢?我们全完了吗?被丢弃了吗?什么也没有留下吗?

弗莱维斯 唉!兄弟们,我应当对你们说些什么话呢?正直的天神可以替我作证,我跟你们一样穷。

仆甲 这样一户人家也会冰消瓦解!这样一位贵主人也会一

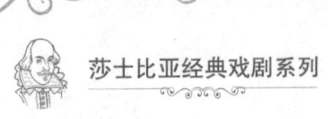

	I am as poor as you.
FIRST SERVANT	Such a house broke?
	So noble a master fall'n? All gone, and not
	One friend to take his fortune by the arm,
	And go along with him?
SECOND SERVANT	As we do turn our backs
	From our companion thrown into his grave,
	So his familiars to his buried fortunes
	Slink all away, leave their false vows with him
	Like empty purses picked; and his poor self,
	A dedicated beggar to the air,
	With his disease of all-shunned poverty,
	Walks like contempt alone. More of our fellows.
	[*Enter other Servants.*]
FLAVIUS	All broken implements of a ruined house.
THIRD SERVANT	Yet do our hearts wear Timon's livery:
	That see I by our faces. We are fellows still,
	Serving alike in sorrow. Leaked is our bark,
	And we, poor mates, stand on the dying deck
	Hearing the surges threat: we must all part
	Into this sea of air.
FLAVIUS	Good fellows all,
	The latest of my wealth I'll share amongst you.
	Wherever we shall meet, for Timon's sake,
	Let's yet be fellows: let's shake our heads and say,
	As 'twere a knell unto our master's fortunes,
	'We have seen better days.' Let each take some [*Offers money.*]
	Nay, put out all your hands. Not one word more.

朝失势！什么都完了！没有一个朋友和他患难相依！

仆乙　正像我们送已死的同伴下葬以后就掉头而去一样，他的知交一见他的财产化为泥土，也就悄悄溜走，只有他们所发的虚伪的誓言，还像一个已经掏空的钱袋似的留在他的身边。可怜的他，变成一个无家可归的叫花子，因为害着一身穷病，弄得人人走避，只好一个人踽踽独行。又有几个我们的弟兄来了。

（其他仆人上）

弗莱维斯　都是一个破落人家的一些破碎的家具。

仆丙　可是我们心里都还穿着泰门发给我们的制服，我们的脸上都流露着眷怀故主的神色。我们现在遭逢不幸，依然是亲密的同伴。我们的大船已经漏了水，我们这些可怜的水手，站在向下沉没的甲板上，听着海涛的威胁；在这茫茫的大海之中，我们必须从此分散了。

弗莱维斯　各位好兄弟们，我愿意把我剩余下来的几个钱分给你们。以后我们无论在什么地方相会，为了泰门的缘故，让我们仍旧都是好朋友；让我们摇摇头，叹口气，悲悼我们主人家业的零落，说，"我们都是曾经见过好日子的。"各人都拿一些去；（给众仆钱）不，大家伸出手来。不必多说，我们现在穷途离别，让悲哀充塞着我们的胸膛吧。（众仆互相拥抱，分别下）啊，

Thus part we rich in sorrow, parting poor.

[*Embrace, and the Servants part several ways.*]

O, the fierce wretchedness that glory brings us!
Who would not wish to be from wealth exempt,
Since riches point to misery and contempt?
Who would be so mocked with glory, or to live,
But in a dream of friendship?
To have his pomp and all what state compounds
But only painted, like his varnished friends?
Poor honest lord, brought low by his own heart,
Undone by goodness! Strange, unusual blood,
When man's worst sin is he does too much good!
Who then dares to be half so kind again?
For bounty, that makes gods, does still mar men.
My dearest lord, blessed to be most accursed,
Rich only to be wretched, thy great fortunes
Are made thy chief afflictions. Alas, kind lord!
He's flung in rage from this ingrateful seat
Of monstrous friends:
Nor has he with him to supply his life,
Or that which can command it.
I'll follow and inquire him out:
I'll ever serve his mind with my best will.
Whilst I have gold, I'll be his steward still. [*Exit.*]

雅典的泰门
TIMON OF ATHENS

荣誉带给我们的残酷的不幸！财富既然只替人招来了困苦和轻蔑，谁还愿意坐拥巨资呢？谁愿意享受片刻的荣华，徒作他人的笑柄？谁愿意在荣华的梦里，相信那些虚伪的友谊？谁还会贪恋那些和趋炎附势的朋友同样不可靠的尊荣豪贵？可怜的老实的大爷！他因为自己心肠太好，所以才到了今天这个地步！谁想得到，一个人行了太多的善事反是最大的罪恶！谁还敢再像他一半仁慈呢？慷慨本来是天神的德性，凡人慷慨了却会损害他自己。我们最亲爱的大爷，你是一个有福之人，却反而成为最倒霉的一个，你的万贯家财害得你如此凄凉，你的富有变成了你的最大的痛苦。唉！仁慈的大爷，他因为气不过这些忘恩负义的朋友，才一怒而去；他既然没有携带活命的资粮，又没有一些可以变换衣食的财帛。我要追寻他的踪迹，尽心竭力侍候他的旨意；当我还有一些金钱在手的时候，我仍然是他的管家。（下）

SCENE III   *Woods and Cave near the Sea-shore.*

[*Enter Timon in the woods.*]

TIMON   [*With a spade.*] O blessèd breeding sun, draw from the earth
Rotten humidity: below thy sister's orb
Infect the air. Twinned brothers of one womb,
Whose procreation, residence, and birth,
Scarce is dividant, touch them with several fortunes,
The greater scorns the lesser. Not nature,
To whom all sores lay siege, can bear great fortune
But by coutempt of nature.
Raise me this beggar, and deny't that lord,
The senators shall bear contempt hereditary,
The beggar native honour.
It is the pasture lards the beggar's sides,
The want that makes him lean. Who dares, who dares
In purity of manhood stand upright
And say 'This man's a flatterer'? If one be,
So are they all, for every grece of fortune
Is smoothed by that below. The learnèd pate
Ducks to the golden fool. All's oblique:
There's nothing level in our cursèd natures
But direct villainy. Therefore be abhorred
All feasts, societies, and throngs of men!
His semblable, yea, himself, Timon disdains.
Destruction fang mankind. Earth, yield me roots.

[*Digs.*]

第三场　海滨附近的树林和岩穴

（泰门自穴中上）

泰　　门　（执铲）神圣的化育万物的太阳啊！把地上的瘴雾吸起，让天空中弥漫着毒气吧！同生同长、同居同宿的孪生兄弟，也让他们各人去接受不同的命运，让那贫贱的人被富贵的人所轻蔑吧。重视伦常天性的人，必须遍受各种颠沛困苦的凌虐；灭伦悖义的人，才会安享荣华。让乞儿跃登高位，大臣退居贱职吧；元老必须世世代代受人蔑视，乞儿必须享受世袭的光荣。有了丰美的牧草，牛儿自然肥胖；缺少了饲料它就会瘦瘠下来。谁敢秉着光明磊落的胸襟挺身而起，说"这人是一个谄媚之徒"？要是有一个人是谄媚之徒，那么谁都是谄媚之徒；因为每一个按照财产多寡区分的阶级，都要被次一阶级所奉承；博学的才人必须向多金的愚夫鞠躬致敬。在我们万恶的天性之中，一切都是歪曲偏斜的，一切都是奸邪淫恶。所以，让我永远厌弃人类的社会吧！泰门憎恨形状像人一样的东西，他也憎恨他自己；愿毁灭吞噬整个人类！泥土，给我一些树根充饥吧！（掘地）谁要是希望你给他一些更

Who seeks for better of thee, sauce his palate
With thy most operant poison! What is here?
[*Discovers gold.*]
Gold? Yellow, glittering, precious gold?
No, gods, I am no idle votarist:
Roots, you clear heavens. Thus much of this will make
Black white, foul fair, wrong right,
Base noble, old young, coward valiant.
Ha, you gods! why this? What this, you gods? Why, this
Will lug your priests and servants from your sides,
Pluck stout men's pillows from below their heads:
This yellow slave
Will knit and break religions, bless th'accursed,
Make the hoar leprosy adored, place thieves
And give them title, knee and approbation
With senators on the bench. This is it
That makes the wappened widow wed again;
She whom the spittle house and ulcerous sores
Would cast the gorge at, this embalms and spices
To th'April day again. Come, damnèd earth,
Thou common whore of mankind, that puts odds
Among the rout of nations, I will make thee
Do thy right nature.
[*March afar off.*]
Ha? A drum? Thou'rt quick,
But yet I'll bury thee: thou'lt go, strong thief, [*Buries the gold.*]
When gouty keepers of thee cannot stand.

好的东西,你就用你最猛烈的毒物餍足他的口味吧!咦,这是什么?(发现金子)金子!黄黄的、发光的、宝贵的金子!不,天神们啊,我不是一个游手好闲的信徒;我只要你们给我一些树根!这东西,只这一点点儿,就可以使黑的变成白的,丑的变成美的,错的变成对的,卑贱变成尊贵,老人变成少年,懦夫变成勇士。嘿!你们这些天神们啊,为什么要给我这东西呢?嘿,这东西会把你们的祭司和仆人从你们的身旁拉走,把壮士头颅底下的枕垫抽去;这黄色的奴隶可以使异教联盟,同宗分裂;它可以使受诅咒的人得福,使害着灰白色的癞病的人为众人所敬爱;它可以使窃贼得到高爵显位,和元老们分庭抗礼;它可以使鸡皮黄脸的寡妇重做新娘,即使她的尊容会使身染恶疮的人见了呕吐,有了这东西也会恢复三春的娇艳。来,该死的土块,你这人尽可夫的娼妇,你惯会在乱七八糟的列国之间挑起纷争,我倒要让你去施展一下你的神通。(远处军队行进声)吓!鼓声吗?你还是活生生的,可是我要把你埋葬了再说。(埋起金子)不,当那看守你的人已经疯癫了的时候,你也许要逃走,

	Nay, stay thou out for earnest. [*Keeps some of the gold.*]
	[*Enter Alcibiades with Drum and Fife, in warlike manner, and Phrynia and Timandra.*]
ALCIBIADES	What art thou there? Speak.
TIMON	A beast, as thou art. The canker gnaw thy heart
	For showing me again the eyes of man!
ALCIBIADES	What is thy name? Is man so hateful to thee
	That art thyself a man?
TIMON	I am Misanthropos, and hate mankind.
	For thy part, I do wish thou wert a dog,
	That I might love thee something.
ALCIBIADES	I know thee well,
	But in thy fortunes am unlearned and strange.
TIMON	I know thee too, and more than that I know thee
	I not desire to know. Follow thy drum,
	With man's blood paint the ground gules, gules.
	Religious canons, civil laws are cruel:
	Then what should war be? This fell whore of thine
	Hath in her more destruction than thy sword,
	For all her cherubin look.
PHRYNIA	Thy lips rot off!
TIMON	I will not kiss thee, then the rot returns
	To thine own lips again.
ALCIBIADES	How came the noble Timon to this change?
TIMON	As the moon does, by wanting light to give.
	But then renew I could not like the moon:
	There were no suns to borrow of.
ALCIBIADES	Noble Timon, what friendship may I do thee?

且待我留着这一些作质。（留下若干金子）

（鼓吹前导，艾西巴第斯戎装率菲莉妮娅、提曼德拉同上）

艾西巴第斯　你是什么？说。

泰　门　我跟你一样是一头野兽。愿蛆虫蛀掉了你的心，因为你又让我看见了人类的面孔！

艾西巴第斯　你叫什么名字？你自己是一个人，怎么把人类恨到这个样子？

泰　门　我是恨世者，一个厌恶人类的人。我倒希望你是一条狗，那么也许我会喜欢你几分。

艾西巴第斯　我认识你是什么人，可是不知道你为什么会变成这样。

泰　门　我也认识你；除了我知道你是什么人之外，我不要再知道什么。跟着你的鼓声去吧；用人类的血染红大地，宗教的戒条、民事的法律，哪一条不是冷酷无情的，那么谁能责怪战争的残酷呢？这一个狠毒的娼妓，虽然瞧上去像个天使一般，杀起人来却比你的刀剑还要厉害呢。

菲莉妮娅　烂掉你的嘴唇！

泰　门　我不要吻你；你的嘴唇是有毒的，让它自己烂掉吧。

艾西巴第斯　尊贵的泰门怎么会变成这个样子？

泰　门　正像月亮一样，因为缺少了可以照人的光；可是我不能一像月亮一样缺而复圆，因为我没有可以借取光明的太阳。

艾西巴第斯　尊贵的泰门，我可以为你做些什么事，来表示友谊呢？

TIMON	None, but to maintain my opinion.
ALCIBIADES	What is it, Timon?
TIMON	Promise me friendship, but perform none: if thou wilt not promise, the gods plague thee, for thou art a man. If thou dost perform, confound thee, for thou art a man.
ALCIBIADES	I have heard in some sort of thy miseries.
TIMON	Thou saw'st them when I had prosperity.
ALCIBIADES	I see them now: then was a blessèd time.
TIMON	As thine is now, held with a brace of harlots.
TIMANDRA	Is this th'Athenian minion whom the world Voiced so regardfully?
TIMON	Art thou Timandra?
TIMANDRA	Yes.
TIMON	Be a whore still. They love thee not that use thee: Give them diseases, leaving with thee their lust. Make use of thy salt hours: season the slaves For tubs and baths, bring down rose-cheeked youth To the tub-fast and the diet.
TIMANDRA	Hang thee, monster!
ALCIBIADES	Pardon him, sweet Timandra, for his wits Are drowned and lost in his calamities. I have but little gold of late, brave Timon, The want whereof doth daily make revolt In my penurious band. I have heard and grieved How cursèd Athens, mindless of thy worth, Forgetting thy great deeds, when neighbour states, But for thy sword and fortune trod upon them—
TIMON	I prithee beat thy drum and get thee gone.
ALCIBIADES	I am thy friend, and pity thee, dear Timon.

泰　　门　不必，只要你支持我的意见。

艾西巴第斯　什么意见，泰门？

泰　　门　用口头上的友谊允许人家，可是不要履行你的允诺；要是你不允许人家，那么神明降祸于你，因为你是一个人！要是你果然履行允诺，那么愿你沉沦地狱，因为你是一个人！

艾西巴第斯　我曾经略微听到过一些你的不幸的遭际。

泰　　门　当我有钱的时候，你就看见过我是怎样不幸了。

焚西巴第斯　我现在才看见你的不幸；当初你是很享福的。

泰　　门　正像你现在一样，给一对娼妓挟住了不放。

提曼德拉　这就是那个受尽世人歌颂的雅典的宠儿吗？

泰　　门　你是提曼德拉吗？

提曼德拉　是的。

泰　　门　做你一辈子的婊子去吧；把你玩弄的那些人并不是真心爱你；他们在你身上发泄过兽欲以后，你就把恶疾传给他们。利用你的淫浪的时间，把他们放进腌缸里或汽浴池中，把那些红颜的少年消磨得形销骨立吧。

提曼德拉　该死的妖魔！

艾西巴第斯　原谅他，好提曼德拉，因为他遭逢变故，他的神智已经混乱了。豪侠的泰门，我近来钱囊羞涩，为了饷糈不足的缘故，我的部队常常发生叛变。我也很痛心，听到那可咒诅的雅典怎样轻视你的才能，忘记你的功德，倘不是靠着你的威名和财力，这区区的雅典城早被强邻鲸食了——

泰　　门　请你敲起鼓来，快点走开吧。

艾西巴第斯　我是你的朋友，我同情你，亲爱的泰门。

TIMON	How dost thou pity him whom thou dost trouble?
	I had rather be alone.
ALCIBIADES	Why, fare thee well:
	Here is some gold for thee.
TIMON	Keep it, I cannot eat it.
ALCIBIADES	When I have laid proud Athens on a heap —
TIMON	Warr'st thou gainst Athens?
ALCIBIADES	Ay, Timon, and have cause.
TIMON	The gods confound them all in thy conquest,
	And thee after, when thou hast conquerèd!
ALCIBIADES	Why me, Timon?
TIMON	That by killing of villains
	Thou wast born to conquer my country.
	Put up thy gold. Go on, here's gold, go on.
	Be as a planetary plague when Jove
	Will o'er some high-viced city hang his poison
	In the sick air. Let not thy sword skip one.
	Pity not honoured age for his white beard:
	He is an usurer. Strike me the counterfeit matron:
	It is her habit only that is honest,
	Herself's a bawd. Let not the virgin's cheek
	Make soft thy trenchant sword, for those milk-paps
	That through the window-bars bore at men's eyes,
	Are not within the leaf of pity writ,
	But set them down horrible traitors. Spare not the babe
	Whose dimpled smiles from fools exhaust their mercy;
	Think it a bastard whom the oracle
	Hath doubtfully pronounced the throat shall cut,
	And mince it *sans* remorse. Swear against objects,

雅典的泰门
TIMON OF ATHENS

泰　　门　你这样跟我胡缠，还说同情我吗？我宁愿一个人在这里。

艾西巴第斯　好，那么再会；这儿有一些金子，你拿去吧。

泰　　门　金子你自己留着，我又不能吃它。

艾西巴第斯　等我把骄傲的雅典踏成平地以后——

泰　　门　你要去打雅典吗？

艾西巴第斯　是的，泰门，我有充分的理由哩。

泰　　门　愿天神降祸于所有的雅典人，让他们一个个在你剑下丧命；等你征服了雅典以后，愿天神再降祸于你！

艾西巴第斯　为什么降祸于我，泰门？

泰　　门　因为天生下你来，要你杀尽那些恶人，征服我的国家。把你的金子藏好了；快去。我这儿还有些金子，也一起给了你吧。快去。愿你奉行天罚，像一颗高悬在作恶多端的城市上的灾星一般，别让你的剑下放过一个人。不要怜悯一把白须的老翁，他是一个放高利贷的人。那凛然不可侵犯的中年妇人，外表上虽然装得十分贞淑，其实却是一个鸨妇，让她死在你的剑下吧。也不要因为处女的秀颊而软下了你的锐利的剑锋；这些惯在窗棂里偷看男人的丫头们，都是可怕的叛徒，不值得怜惜。也不要饶过婴孩，像一个傻子似的看见他的浮着酒窝的微笑而大发慈悲；你应当认为他是一个私生子，上天已经向你隐约预示他将来长大以后会割断你的咽喉，所以你必须硬着心肠把他剁死。你的耳

	Put armour on thine ears and on thine eyes
	Whose proof nor yells of mothers, maids, nor babes,
	Nor sight of priests in holy vestments bleeding,
	Shall pierce a jot. [*Offers gold.*] There's gold to pay
	thy soldiers:
	Make large confusion, and, thy fury spent,
	Confounded be thyself. Speak not, be gone.
ALCIBIADES	[*Takes gold.*] Hast thou gold yet? I'll take the gold thou givest me,
	Not all thy counsel.
TIMON	Dost thou or dost thou not, heaven's curse upon thee!
PHRYNIA TIMANDRA	Give us some gold, good Timon. Hast thou more?
TIMON	Enough to make a whore forswear her trade,
	And to make whores, a bawd. Hold up, you sluts,
	Your aprons mountant. [*Throws gold into their aprons.*]
	You are not oathable,
	Although I know you'll swear, terribly swear
	Into strong shudders and to heavenly agues
	Th 'immortal gods that hear you. Spare your oaths:
	I'll trust to your conditions. Be whores still,
	And he whose pious breath seeks to convert you,
	Be strong in whore, allure him, burn him up:
	Let your close fire predominate his smoke,
	And be no turncoats. Yet may your pains six months
	Be quite contrary, and thatch your poor thin roofs
	With burdens of the dead — some that were hanged,
	No matter. Wear them, betray with them, whore still,
	Paint till a horse may mire upon your face.

朵上，眼睛上，都要罩着一重厚甲，让你听不到母亲，少女和婴孩们的啼哭，看不见披着圣服的祭司的流血。（拿出金子）把这些金子拿去分给你的兵士们，让他们去造成一次大大的纷乱；等你的盛怒消释以后，愿你也不得好死！不必多说，快去。

艾西巴第斯　（接过金子）你还有金子吗？我愿意接受你给我的金子，可是不能完全接受你的劝告。

泰　　　门　接受也好，不接受也好，愿上天的咒诅降在你身上！

菲莉妮娅
提曼德拉　　好泰门，给我们一些金子；你还有吗？

泰　　　门　有，有，有，我有足够的金子，可以使一个妓女改业，自己当起老鸨来。揭起你们的裙子来，你们这两个贱婢。（向其裙兜里一扔金子）你们是不配发誓的，虽然我知道你们发起誓来，听见你们的天神也会浑身发抖，毛骨悚然；不要发什么誓了，我愿意信任你们。做你们一辈子的婊子吧；要是有什么仁人君子，想要劝你们改邪归正，你们就得施展你们的狐媚伎俩引诱他，使他在欲火里丧身。一辈子做你们的婊子吧；你们的

	A pox of wrinkles!
PHRYNIA } TIMANDRA	Well, More gold: what then? Believe't that we'll do anything for gold.
TIMON	Consumptions sow

  In hollow bones of man, strike their sharp shins,
  And mar men's spurring. Crack the lawyer's voice,
  That he may never more false title plead,
  Nor sound his quillets shrilly. Hoar the flamen
  That scolds against the quality of flesh,
  And not believes himself. Down with the nose,
  Down with it flat: take the bridge quite away
  Of him that, his particular to foresee,
  Smells from the general weal. Make curled-pate ruffians bald,
  And let the unscarred braggarts of the war
  Derive some pain from you. Plague all,
  That your activity may defeat and quell
  The source of all erection. There's more gold.
  Do you damn others, and let this damn you,
  And ditches grave you all!

PHRYNIA } TIMANDRA	More counsel with more money, bounteous Timon.
TIMON	More whore, more mischief first: I have given you earnest.
ALCIBIADES	Strike up the drum towards Athens!— Farewell, Timon: If I thrive well, I'll visit thee again.
TIMON	If I hope well, I'll never see thee more.
ALCIBIADES	I never did thee harm.

脸上必须满涂着脂粉，让马蹄踏上去都会拔不出来。

菲莉妮娅
提曼德拉　好，再给我们一些金子。还有什么吩咐？相信我们，只要有金子，我们是什么都愿意干的。

泰　　门　把痨病的种子播在人们枯干的骨髓里；让他们胫骨疯瘫，不能上马驰驱。嘶哑了律师的喉咙，让他不再颠倒黑白，为非分的权利辩护，鼓弄他的如簧之舌。叫那痛斥肉体的情欲、自己不相信自己的话的祭司害起满身的癞病；叫那长着尖锐的鼻子、一味钻营逐利的家伙烂去了鼻子；叫那长着一头鬈曲秀发的光棍变成秃子；叫那不曾受过伤，光会吹牛的战士也从你们身上受到一些痛苦；让所有的人都被你们害得身败名裂。再给你们一些金子；你们去害了别人，再让这东西来害你们，愿你们一起倒在阴沟里死去！

菲莉妮娅
提曼德拉　宽宏慷慨的泰门，再给我们一些金子吧，你还有什么话要对我们说呢？

泰　　门　你们先去多卖几次淫，多害几个人，回头来我还有金子给你们。

艾西巴第斯　敲起鼓来，向雅典进发！再会，泰门；要是我此去能够成功，我会再来访问你的。

泰　　门　要是我的希望没有落空，我再也不要看见你了。

艾西巴第斯　我从来没有得罪过你。

TIMON	Yes, thou spok'st well of me.
ALCIBIADES	Call'st thou that harm?
TIMON	Men daily find it. Get thee away, and take Thy beagles with thee.
ALCIBIADES	We but offend him. Strike!

[*Drums beat. Exeunt all but Timon.*]

TIMON That nature, being sick of man's unkindness,
Should yet be hungry! Common mother, thou [*Digs.*]
Whose womb unmeasurable and infinite breast
Teems and feeds all, whose selfsame mettle,
Whereof thy proud child, arrogant man, is puffed,
Engenders the black toad and adder blue,
The gilded newt and eyeless venomed worm,
With all th'abhorrèd births below crisp heaven
Whereon Hyperion's quick'ning fire doth shine —
Yield him, who all thy human sons do hate,
From forth thy plenteous bosom one poor root.
Ensear thy fertile and conceptious womb:
Let it no more bring out ingrateful man.
Go great with tigers, dragons, wolves, and bears,
Teem with new monsters whom thy upward face
Hath to the marbled mansion all above
Never presented! [*Finds a root.*] O, a root. Dear thanks!
Dry up thy marrows, vines, and plough-torn leas,
Whereof ingrateful man, with liquorish draughts
And morsels unctuous greases his pure mind,
That from it all consideration slips!

[*Enter Apemantus.*]

More man? Plague, plague!

泰　　门　可是你说过我的好话。

艾西巴第斯　这难道对你是有害的吗？

泰　　门　人们每天都可以发现说好话的人总是不怀好意。走开，把你这两条小猎狗带了去。

艾西巴第斯　我们留在这儿反而惹他生气。敲鼓！（敲鼓；除泰门外全下）

泰　　门　想不到在饱尝人世的无情之后，还会感到饥饿；你万物之母啊，（掘地）你的不可限量的胸腹，孳乳着繁育着一切；你的精气不但把傲慢的人类，你的骄儿，吹嘘长大，也同样生养了黑色的蟾蜍、青色的蝮蛇、金甲的蝾螈、盲目的毒虫以及一切光天化日之下可憎可厌的生物；请你从你那丰饶的怀里，把一块粗硬的树根给那痛恨你一切人类子女的我果果腹吧！枯萎了你的肥沃多产的子宫，让它不要再生出负心的人类来！愿你怀孕着虎龙狼熊，以及一切宇宙覆载之中所未见的妖禽怪兽！（发现一树根）啊！一个根；谢谢。干涸了你的血液，枯焦了你的土壤；忘恩负义的人类，都是靠着你的供给，用酒肉腻塞了他的良心，以致迷失了一切的理性！

（艾帕曼特斯上）

又有人来了！该死！该死！

APEMANTUS	I was directed hither. Men report
	Thou dost affect my manners, and dost use them.
TIMON	'Tis then because thou dost not keep a dog,
	Whom I would imitate. Consumption catch thee!
APEMANTUS	This is in thee a nature but infected,
	A poor unmanly melancholy sprung
	From change of fortune. Why this spade? This place?
	This slave-like habit? And these looks of care?
	Thy flatterers yet wear silk, drink wine, lie soft,
	Hug their diseased perfumes, and have forgot
	That ever Timon was. Shame not these woods
	By putting on the cunning of a carper.
	Be thou a flatterer now, and seek to thrive
	By that which has undone thee; hinge thy knee
	And let his very breath whom thou'lt observe
	Blow off thy cap: praise his most vicious strain,
	And call it excellent. Thou wast told thus:
	Thou gav'st thine ears, like tapsters that bade welcome,
	To knaves and all approachers. 'Tis most just
	That thou turn rascal: hadst thou wealth again,
	Rascals should have't. Do not assume my likeness.
TIMON	Were I like thee, I'd throw away myself.
APEMANTUS	Thou hast cast away thyself being like thyself:
	A madman so long, now a fool. What, think'st
	That the bleak air, thy boisterous chamberlain
	Will put thy shirt on warm? Will these moist trees,
	That have outlived the eagle page thy heels
	And skip when thou point'st out? Will the cold brook,
	Candied with ice, caudle thy morning taste

雅典的泰门
TIMON OF ATHENS

艾帕曼特斯　人家指点我到这儿来；他们说你学会了我的举止，模仿着我的行为。

泰　　门　因为你还不曾养一条狗，否则我倒宁愿学它；愿瘟病抓了你去！

艾帕曼特斯　你这种样子不过是一时的感触，因为命运的转移而发生的怯懦的忧郁。为什么拿起这柄锄头？为什么住在这个地方？为什么穿上这身奴才的装束？为什么露出这样忧伤的神色？向你献媚的家伙现在还穿的是绸缎，喝的是美酒，睡的是温软的被褥，彻底忘记了世上曾经有过一个名叫泰门的人。不要装出一副骂世者的腔调，害这些山林蒙羞吧。还是自己也去做一个献媚的人，在那些毁荡了你的家产的家伙手下讨生活吧。弯下你的膝头，让他嘴里的气息吹去你的帽子；尽管他发着怎样大的脾气，你都要把他恭维得五体投地。你应当像笑脸迎人的酒保一样，倾听着每一个流氓恶棍的话；你必须自己也做一个恶棍，要是你再发了财，也不过让恶棍们享用了去。可不要再学着我的样子啦。

泰　　门　要是我像了你，我宁愿把自己丢掉。

艾帕曼特斯　你因为像你自己，早已把你自己丢掉了；你做了这么久的疯人，现在却变成了一个傻子。怎么！你以为那凛冽的霜风，你那喧嚷的仆人，会把你的衬衫烘暖吗？这些寿命超过鹰隼、罩满苍苔的老树，会追随你的左右，听候你的使唤吗？那冰冻的寒溪会替你在清晨煮好粥

	To cure thy o'ernight's surfeit? Call the creatures
	Whose naked natures live in all the spite
	Of wreakful heaven, whose bare unhousèd trunks
	To the conflicting elements exposed
	Answer mere nature: bid them flatter thee.
	O, thou shalt find —
TIMON	— a fool of thee. Depart.
APEMANTUS	I love thee better now than e'er I did.
TIMON	I hate thee worse.
APEMANTUS	Why?
TIMON	Thou flatter'st misery.
APEMANTUS	I flatter not, but say thou art a caitiff.
TIMON	Why dost thou seek me out?
APEMANTUS	To vex thee.
TIMON	Always a villain's office or a fool's. Dost please thyself in't?
APEMANTUS	Ay.
TIMON	What, a knave too?
APEMANTUS	If thou didst put this sour cold habit on
	To castigate thy pride, 't were well: but thou
	Dost it enforcèdly. Thou'dst courtier be again,
	Wert thou not beggar. Willing misery
	Outlives incertain pomp, is crowned before:
	The one is filling still, never complete;
	The other, at high wish. Best state, contentless,
	Hath a distracted and most wretched being,
	Worse than the worst, content.
	Thou shouldst desire to die, being miserable.
TIMON	Not by his breath that is more miserable.

汤，替你消除昨夜的积食吗？叫那些赤裸裸地生存在上天的暴怒之中，无遮无掩地受着风吹雨打霜雪侵凌的草木向你献媚吧；啊！你就会知道——

泰　　门　你是一个傻子。快去。

艾帕曼特斯　我从来不曾像现在这样喜欢过你。

泰　　门　我从来不曾像现在这样讨厌过你。

艾帕曼特斯　为什么？

泰　　门　因为你向贫困献媚。

艾帕曼特斯　我没有献媚，我说你是一个下流的恶汉。

泰　　门　为什么你要来找我？

艾帕曼特斯　因为我要惹你恼怒。

泰　　门　这是一个恶徒或者愚人的工作。你以为惹人家恼怒对于你自己是一件乐事吗？

艾帕曼特斯　是的。

泰　　门　怎么！你又是一个无赖吗？

艾帕曼特斯　要是你披上这身寒酸的衣服，目的只是要惩罚你自己的骄傲，那么很好；可是你是出于勉强的，倘然你不再是一个乞丐，你就会再去做一个廷臣。自愿的贫困胜如不定的浮华；穷奢极欲的人要是贪得无厌，比最贫困而知足的人更要不幸得多了。你既然这样困苦，应该但求速死。

泰　　门　我不会听了一个比我更倒霉的人的话而去寻死。你是

Thou art a slave whom Fortune's tender arm
With favour never clasped, but bred a dog.
Hadst thou like us from our first swath proceeded
The sweet degrees that this brief world affords
To such as may the passive drugs of it
Freely command, thou wouldst have plunged thyself
In general riot, melted down thy youth
In different beds of lust, and never learned
The icy precepts of respect, but followed
The sugared game before thee. But myself,
Who had the world as my confectionary,
The mouths, the tongues, the eyes and hearts of men
At duty, more than I could frame employment,
That numberless upon me stuck as leaves
Do on the oak, have with one winter's brush
Fell from their boughs and left me open, bare
For every storm that blows: I, to bear this,
That never knew but better, is some burden.
Thy nature did commence in sufferance, time
Hath made thee hard in't. Why shouldst thou hate men?
They never flattered thee. What hast thou given?
If thou wilt curse, thy father, that poor rag,
Must be thy subject, who in spite put stuff
To some she beggar and compounded thee
Poor rogue hereditary. Hence, be gone!
If thou hadst not been born the worst of men,
Thou hadst been a knave and flatterer.

APEMANTUS Art thou proud yet?
TIMON Ay, that I am not thee.

一个奴隶,命运的温柔的手臂从来不曾拥抱过你。要是你从呱呱坠地的时候就跟我们一样,可以随心所欲地享受这浮世的欢娱,你一定已经沉溺在无边的放荡里,把你的青春消磨在左拥右抱之中,除了一味追求眼前的淫乐以外,再也不会知道那些冷冰冰的人伦道德。可是我,整个的世界曾经是我的糖果的作坊;人们的嘴、舌头、眼睛和心都争先恐后地等候着我的使唤,虽然我没有这许多工作可以给他们做;无数的人像叶子依附橡树一般依附着我,可是经不起冬风的一吹,他们便落下枝头,剩下我赤裸裸的枯干,去忍受风雨的摧残;像我这样享福过来的人,一旦挨受这种逆运,那才是一件难堪的重荷;你却是从开始时候就尝到人世的痛苦的,经验已经把你磨炼得十分坚强了。你为什么厌恶人类呢?他们从来没有向你献过媚;你曾经有些什么东西给人家呢?倘然你要咒骂,你就得咒骂你的父亲,那个穷酸的叫花子,他因为一时兴起,和一个女乞婆养下了你这世袭的穷光蛋来。滚开!快去!倘然你不是生下来就是世间最下贱的人,你就是个奸佞的小人。

艾帕曼特斯　你现在还是这样骄傲吗?
泰　　　门　是的,因为我不是你而骄傲。

APEMANTUS	I, that I was no prodigal.
TIMON	I, that I am one now.
	Were all the wealth I have shut up in thee
	I'd give thee leave to hang it. Get thee gone.
	That the whole life of Athens were in this!
	Thus would I eat it. [*Eats a root.*]
APEMANTUS	Here, I will mend thy feast. [*Offers food.*]
TIMON	First mend my company: take away thyself.
APEMANTUS	So I shall mend mine own, by th'lack of thine.
TIMON	'Tis not well mended so, it is but botched;
	If not, I would it were.
APEMANTUS	What wouldst thou have to Athens?
TIMON	Thee thither in a whirlwind. If thou wilt,
	Tell them there I have gold. [*Shows gold.*] Look, so I have.
APEMANTUS	Here is no use for gold.
TIMON	The best and truest,
	For here it sleeps, and does no hirèd harm.
APEMANTUS	Where liest a-nights, Timon?
TIMON	Under that's above me.
	Where feed'st thou a-days, Apemantus?
APEMANTUS	Where my stomach finds meat, or rather, where I eat it.
TIMON	Would poison were obedient and knew my mind!
APEMANTUS	Where wouldst thou send it?
TIMON	To sauce thy dishes.
APEMANTUS	The middle of humanity thou never knewest, but the extremity of both ends. When thou wast in thy gilt and thy perfume, they mocked thee for too much curiosity: in thy rags thou know'st none, but art despised for the

雅典的泰门
TIMON OF ATHENS

艾帕曼特斯　我也因为我不是一个浪子而骄傲。

泰　　门　我因为现在是个浪子而骄傲。要是我所有的一切钱财都在你的手掌之中，我也不向你要。快去！但愿全体雅典人的生命都在这块根里，我要把它像这样一口吞下！（食树根）

艾帕曼特斯　给你，我要提高你的宴席的档次。（递食物）

泰　　门　先提高我的宾客的档次吧，你不配在这里，走开！

艾帕曼特斯　我总归要比你那帮损友强。

泰　　门　未必如此，你跟他们是龟蛇一窝，即使不是龟蛇一窝，在我看来也差不多。

艾帕曼特斯　你要我带些什么去给雅典人？

泰　　门　但愿一阵旋风把你卷到雅典去。要是你愿意，你可以告诉他们我这儿有金子；瞧，我有金子。（展示金子）

艾帕曼特斯　你在这儿用不着金子。

泰　　门　金子在这儿才是最好最真的，因为它安安静静地躺在这儿，不被人利用去为非作歹。

艾帕曼特斯　晚上在什么地方睡觉，泰门？

泰　　门　在太虚的覆罩之下。你白天在什么地方吃东西，艾帕曼特斯？

艾帕曼特斯　在我的肚子找到肉食的地方；或者说，在我吃东西的地方。

泰　　门　我希望鸩毒服从我的意志！

艾帕曼特斯　你要把它送到什么地方去？

泰　　门　撒在你的食物里。

艾帕曼特斯　你只知道人生中的两个极端，不曾度过中庸的生活。当你锦衣美服、麝香熏身的时候，他们讥笑你的繁文

	contrary. There's a medlar for thee, eat it.
TIMON	On what I hate I feed not.
APEMANTUS	Dost hate a medlar?
TIMON	Ay, though it look like thee.
APEMANTUS	An th'hadst hated meddlers sooner, thou shouldst have loved thyself better now. What man didst thou ever know unthrift that was beloved after his means?
TIMON	Who, without those means thou talk'st of, didst thou ever know beloved?
APEMANTUS	Myself.
TIMON	I understand thee: thou hadst some means to keep a dog.
APEMANTUS	What things in the world canst thou nearest compare to thy flatterers?
TIMON	Women nearest, but men, men are the things themselves. What wouldst thou do with the world, Apemantus, if it lay in thy power?
APEMANTUS	Give it the beasts, to be rid of the men.
TIMON	Wouldst thou have thyself fall in the confusion of men, and remain a beast with the beasts?
APEMANTUS	Ay, Timon.
TIMON	A beastly ambition, which the gods grant thee t'attain to. If thou wert the lion, the fox would beguile thee: if thou wert the lamb, the fox would eat thee: if thou wert the fox, the lion would suspect thee when peradventure thou wert accused by the ass; if thou wert the ass: thy dulness would torment thee, and still thou livedst but as a breakfast to the wolf. If thou wert the wolf, thy greediness would afflict thee, and oft thou shouldst

		缛礼；现在你不衫不履，敝首垢面，他们又蔑视你的落拓疏狂。这里有一个欧楂果，给你吃了吧。
泰	门	我恨欧楂，我不吃。
艾帕曼特斯		恨欧楂？
泰	门	对，因为它又酸又烂，看起来像你。
艾帕曼特斯		如果你早一点恨那些糜烂的人渣，你现在会更加自爱。你可知，哪一个富豪在家财败尽之后，还会受人尊崇？
泰	门	我可知，哪一个人并没有你所说的家财，但依旧受人爱戴？
艾帕曼特斯		我自己就是。
泰	门	我知道你的意思，一条狗你还是养得起的，你再穷，狗也对你摇尾乞怜。
艾帕曼特斯		你把向你献媚的人比作世间什么东西？
泰	门	艾帕曼特斯，要是全世界俯伏在你的脚下，你预备把它怎样处置？
艾帕曼特斯		把它送给野兽，吃尽了所有的人类。
泰	门	你愿意置身于人类的混乱之中，而与众兽为伍，做一头畜生吗？
艾帕曼特斯		是的，泰门。
泰	门	愿天神保佑你达到这一个畜生的愿望。要是你做了狮子，狐狸会来欺骗你；要是你做了羔羊，狐狸会来吃了你，要是你做了狐狸，万一驴子把你告发，狮子会对你起疑心；要是你做了驴子，你的愚蠢将使你受苦，而且你也不免做豺狼的一顿早餐；要是你做了狼，你的贪馋将使你烦恼，而且常常要为着求食而冒生命的

hazard thy life for thy dinner. Wert thou the unicorn, pride and wrath would confound thee and make thine own self the conquest of thy fury: wert thou a bear, thou wouldst be killed by the horse: wert thou a horse, thou wouldst be seized by the leopard: wert thou a leopard, thou wert german to the lion and the spots of thy kindred were jurors on thy life: all thy safety were remotion and thy defence absence. What beast couldst thou be that were not subject to a beast? And what beast art thou already, that see'st not thy loss in transformation!

APEMANTUS If thou couldst please me with speaking to me, thou mightst have hit upon it here: the commonwealth of Athens is become a forest of beasts.

TIMON How has the ass broke the wall, that thou art out of the city?

APEMANTUS Yonder comes a poet and a painter. The plague of company light upon thee! I will fear to catch it and give way. When I know not what else to do, I'll see thee again.

TIMON When there is nothing living but thee, thou shalt be welcome. I had rather be a beggar's dog than Apemantus.

APEMANTUS Thou art the cap of all the fools alive.

TIMON Would thou wert clean enough to spit upon.

APEMANTUS A plague on thee! Thou art too bad to curse.

TIMON All villains that do stand by thee are pure.

APEMANTUS There is no leprosy but what thou speak'st.

TIMON If I name thee.

危险；要是你做了犀牛，你的骄傲和凶暴将使你受罪，让你自己被你的盛怒所克服，要是你做了熊，你要死在马蹄的践踏之下；要是你做了马，你要被豹子所攫噬；要是你做了豹，你是狮子的近亲，你身上的斑纹将使你送命。你没有安全，没有保障。你要做一头什么野兽，才可以不受别的野兽的侵害呢？你不知道你现在已经是一头什么野兽，你在变形以后将要遭到怎样的不幸。

艾帕曼特斯 你这番话讲得倒很有理；雅典已经变成一个众兽群居的林薮了。

泰　　门 那么驴子是怎样冲破了城墙，让你溜到城外来的？

艾帕曼特斯 那里有一个诗人和一个画师来了；愿来来往往的人们把你缠扰得不得安宁！我可要敬谢不敏，抽身远避了。当我不知道还有什么事情可做的时候，我会再来瞧你的。

泰　　门 当世间除了你之外死得什么都不剩的时候，我会欢迎你的。我宁愿做乞丐手里牵着的狗，也不愿做艾帕曼特斯。

艾帕曼特斯 你是世上天字第一号的大傻瓜。

泰　　门 我希望你再干净点儿，可以让我把唾液吐在你身上！

艾帕曼特斯 愿你遭瘟！你太坏了，我简直不屑咒你！

泰　　门 所有的恶人站在你身边，相形之下也会变成正人君子。

艾帕曼特斯 你一说话，嘴里也会掉下癞病来。

泰　　门 要是我再提起你的名字的话。倘不是怕污了我的手，我早就打你了。去，你这癞狗生的杂种！世上会有你

APEMANTUS	I'll beat thee, but I should infect my hands.
	I would my tongue could rot them off!
TIMON	Away, thou issue of a mangy dog!
	Choler does kill me that thou art alive.
	I swoon to see thee.
APEMANTUS	Would thou wouldst burst!
TIMON	Away, thou tedious rogue!
	I am sorry I shall lose a stone by thee. [*Throws a stone at him.*]
APEMANTUS	Beast!
TIMON	Slave!
APEMANTUS	Toad!
TIMON	Rogue, rogue, rogue!

I am sick of this false world, and will love nought
But even the mere necessities upon't.
Then, Timon, presently prepare thy grave:
Lie where the light foam of the sea may beat
Thy gravestone daily. Make thine epitaph,
That death in me at others' lives may laugh. —
  [*To the gold.*] O thou sweet king-killer, and dear divorce
'Twixt natural son and sire: thou bright defiler
Of Hymen's purest bed, thou valiant Mars,
Thou ever young, fresh, loved and delicate wooer,
Whose blush doth thaw the consecrated snow
That lies on Dian's lap: thou visible god,
That sold'rest close impossibilities
And mak'st them kiss; that speak'st with every tongue,
To every purpose! O thou touch of hearts:

艾帕曼特斯	这样的人活着,把我气也气死了;我一见了你就要气昏了脑袋。
艾帕曼特斯	但愿我能口吐咒语,把你的双手烂掉。
泰门	去!你这癞狗生的杂种!世上会有你这样的人活着,把我气也气死了;我一见了你就要气昏了脑袋。
艾帕曼特斯	我希望你会气破了肚子!
泰门	去,你这讨厌的混蛋!算我倒霉,还要赔一块石子来扔你。(向艾帕曼特斯掷石)
艾帕曼特斯	畜生!
泰门	奴才!
艾帕曼特斯	蛤蟆!
泰门	混蛋,混蛋,混蛋!我讨厌这个虚伪的世界和这个世界上所有的一切。所以,泰门,赶快预备你的坟墓吧;安息在海水的泡沫可以每天打击你的墓碣的地方;刻下你的墓志铭,让你的一死讥刺着世人的偷生苟活。(视金)啊,你可爱的凶手,帝王逃不过你的掌握,亲生的父子会被你离间!你灿烂的奸夫,淫污了纯洁的婚床!你勇敢的战神!你永远年轻韶秀、永远被人爱恋的娇美的情郎,你的羞颜可以融化了狄安娜女神膝上的冰雪!你有形的神明,你会使冰炭化为胶漆,仇敌互相亲吻!你会说任何的方言,使每一个人唯命是从!

APEMANTUS	Think thy slave man rebels, and by thy virtue Set them into confounding odds, that beasts May have the world in empire. Would 't were so! But not till I am dead. I'll say th'hast gold: Thou wilt be thronged to shortly.
TIMON	Thronged to?
APEMANTUS	Ay.
TIMON	Thy back, I prithee.
APEMANTUS	[*Begins to leave.*] Live, and love thy misery.
TIMON	Long live so, and so die. — I am quit.
APEMANTUS	More things like men! Eat, Timon, and abhor them.
	[*Exit Apemantus.*]
	[*Enter the Banditti.*]
FIRST BANDIT	Where should he have this gold? It is some poor fragment, some slender ort of his remainder: the mere want of gold, and the falling-from of his friends, drove him into this melancholy.
SECOND BANDIT	It is noised he hath a mass of treasure.
THIRD BANDIT	Let us make the assay upon him: if he care not for 't, he will supply us easily: if he covetously reserve it, how shall's get it?
SECOND BANDIT	True, for he bears it not about him: 'tis hid.
FIRST BANDIT	Is not this he?
OTHER BANDITTI	Where?
SECOND BANDIT	'Tis his description.
THIRD BANDIT	He, I know him.
ALL BANDITTI	[*They come forward.*] Save thee, Timon!
TIMON	Now, thieves.

你动人心坎的宝物啊！你的奴隶，那些人类，要造反了，快快运用你的法力，让他们互相砍杀，留下这个世界来给兽类统治吧。

艾帕曼特斯 但愿如此；可是等我死了再说。我要去对他们说你有金子；不久他们就要蜂拥而来了。

泰　　门 蜂拥而来？

艾帕曼特斯 正是。

泰　　门 请你快给我滚开。

艾帕曼特斯 （欲走）活下去，喜爱你的困苦吧！（下）

泰　　门 好容易把他赶走了。又有些像人一样的东西来啦！真讨厌。

艾帕曼特斯 又有一些像人一样的东西来了！吃掉他们吧，泰门，可恶的东西。（艾帕曼特斯下）

（众窃贼上）

贼　　甲 他哪里来的这些金子？那一定是他剩在身边的一些碎片零屑。他就是因为囊中金罄，友朋离散，所以才发起疯来的。

贼　　乙 听说他还有许多宝贝。

贼　　丙 让我们吓唬他一下：要是他不爱惜金银，一定会双手捧给我们的；要是他推推托托不肯交出来，那便怎么办呢？

贼　　乙 不错，他并不把它们放在身边，定是藏得好好的。

贼　　甲 这不就是他吗？

众　　贼 在哪儿？

贼　　乙 正是他的样子。

贼　　丙 他；我认识是他。

众　　贼 （众贼上前）你好，泰门？

BANDITTI	Soldiers, not thieves.
TIMON	Both too, and women's sons.
BANDITTI	We are not thieves, but men that much do want.
TIMON	Your greatest want is, you want much of meat.
	Why should you want? Behold, the earth hath roots;
	Within this mile break forth a hundred springs:
	The oaks bear mast, the briers scarlet hips:
	The bounteous housewife nature on each bush
	Lays her full mess before you. Want? Why want?
FIRST BANDIT	We cannot live on grass, on berries, water,
	As beasts and birds and fishes.
TIMON	Nor on the beasts themselves, the birds, and fishes;
	You must eat men. Yet thanks I must you con
	That you are thieves professed, that you work not
	In holier shapes; for there is boundless theft
	In limited professions. Rascal thieves,
	Here's gold. Go, suck the subtle blood o'th' grape,
	Till the high fever seethe your blood to froth,
	And so scape hanging. Trust not the physician,
	His antidotes are poison, and he slays
	More than you rob. Take wealth and lives together:
	Do, villains, do, since you protest to do't,
	Like workmen. I'll example you with thievery.
	The sun's a thief, and with his great attraction
	Robs the vast sea: the moon's an arrant thief,
	And her pale fire she snatches from the sun:
	The sea's a thief, whose liquid surge resolves
	The moon into salt tears: the earth's a thief,
	That feeds and breeds by a composture stolen

| 泰 | 门 | 好哇,你们这些偷儿? |

| 众 | 贼 | 我们是兵士,不是偷儿。 |

| 泰 | 门 | 是兵士,也是偷儿;你们都是妇人的儿子。 |

| 众 | 贼 | 我们不是偷儿,不过是些什么都没有的穷光蛋。 |

| 泰 | 门 | 你们没有东西吃吗?为什么没有?瞧,地下生着各种草木的根;在这一英里以内,长着多少的山蔬野草;橡树上长着橡果,野蔷薇也长着一粒粒红色的果实;那慷慨的主妇,大自然,在每一棵植物上替你们安排好美食,你们还嫌没有东西吃吗? |

| 贼 | 甲 | 我们不能像鸟兽游鱼一样,靠着吃草啄果,喝些清水过活呀。 |

| 泰 | 门 | 你们也不能靠着吃鸟兽游鱼的肉过活;你们是一定要吃人的。可是我还是要谢谢你们,因为你们都是明目张胆地做贼,并不蒙着庄严神圣的假面具;那些道貌岸然的正人君子,才是最可怕的穿窬大盗哩。你们这些鼠贼,拿着这些金子去吧。去,痛痛快快地喝个醉,让烈酒烧枯你们的血液,免得你们到绞架上去受苦。不要相信医生的话,他的药方上都是毒药,他杀死的比你们偷窃的还多。放手偷吧,尽情杀吧;你们既然做了贼,尽管把恶事当作正当的工作一样做去吧。我可以讲几个最大的窃贼给你们听:太阳是个贼,用他

	From gen'ral excrement: each thing's a thief.
	The laws, your curb and whip, in their rough power
	Have unchecked theft. Love not yourselves, away!
	Rob one another: there's more gold. Cut throats:
	All that you meet are thieves. To Athens go,
	Break open shops: nothing can you steal
	But thieves do lose it. Steal less for this I give you,
	And gold confound you howsoe'er! Amen.
THIRD BANDIT	Has almost charmed me from my profession by persuading me to it.
FIRST BANDIT	'Tis in the malice of mankind that he thus advises us, not to have us thrive in our mystery.
SECOND BANDIT	I'll believe him as an enemy, and give over my trade.
FIRST BANDIT	Let us first see peace in Athens: there is no time so miserable but a man may be true. [*Exeunt Thieves.*]
	[*Enter the Steward to Timon.*]
FLAVIUS	O you gods!
	Is yond despised and ruinous man my lord?
	Full of decay and failing? O monument
	And wonder of good deeds evilly bestowed!
	What an alteration of honour
	Has desp'rate want made!
	What viler thing upon the earth than friends
	Who can bring noblest minds to basest ends!
	How rarely does it meet with this time's guise,
	When man was wished to love his enemies!
	Grant I may ever love and rather woo
	Those that would mischief me than those that do!

雅典的泰门
TIMON OF ATHENS

的伟大的吸力偷窃海上的潮水；月亮是个无耻的贼，她的惨白的光辉是从太阳那儿偷来的；海是个贼，他的汹涌的潮汐把月亮溶化成咸的眼泪；地是个贼，他偷了万物的粪便作肥料，使自己肥沃；什么都是贼，那束缚你们鞭打你们的法律，也凭借它的野蛮的威力，实行不受约制的偷窃。不要爱你们自己，快去！各人互相偷窃。再拿一些金子去吧。放大胆子去杀人；你们所碰到的人没有一个不是贼。到雅典去，打开人家的店铺；你们所偷到的东西没有一件本来不是贼赃。不要因为我给了你们金子就不去做贼；让金子送了你们的性命！阿门。

贼 丙 他劝我做贼，反而把我说得不愿意做贼了。

贼 甲 他因为痛恨人类，所以这样劝告我们；他不是希望我们靠着做贼发财享福。

贼 乙 我要把他的话当作仇敌的话，放弃我的本行了。

贼 甲 让我们替雅典维持治安；无论时世怎样艰难，一个人总可以安分度日的。（众贼下）

（弗莱维斯上）

弗莱维斯 天哪！那个衣服褴褛、形容枯槁的人，便是我的主人吗？他怎么会衰落到这个地步？为善的人竟会得到这样的恶报！从前那样炙手可热，一朝穷了下来，就要受尽世人的冷眼！世上还有什么东西比那些把最高贵的人引到了最没落的下场的朋友们更可恶的！在这样尔虞我诈的人间，一个人与其爱他的朋友，还不如爱他的仇敌；虽然仇敌对我不怀好意，可是朋友却在实际上陷害我。他已经看见我了。我要向他表示我的真

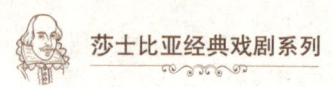

	Has caught me in his eye: I will present
	My honest grief unto him; and as my lord
	Still serve him with my life. — My dearest master!
	[*Timon comes forward.*]
TIMON	Away! What art thou?
FLAVIUS	Have you forgot me, sir?
TIMON	Why dost ask that? I have forgot all men:
	Then, if thou grant'st thou'rt a man, I have forgot thee.
FLAVIUS	An honest poor servant of yours.
TIMON	Then I know thee not.
	I never had honest man about me: ay, all
	I kept were knaves to serve in meat to villains.
FLAVIUS	[*Weeps.*] The gods are witness,
	Ne'er did poor steward wear a truer grief
	For his undone lord than mine eyes for you.
TIMON	What, dost thou weep? Come nearer. Then I love thee
	Because thou art a woman, and disclaim'st
	Flinty mankind whose eyes do never give
	But thorough lust and laughter. Pity's sleeping:
	Strange times, that weep with laughing, not with weeping!
FLAVIUS	I beg of you to know me, good my lord,
	T'accept my grief and whilst this poor wealth lasts
	To entertain me as your steward still.
TIMON	Had I a steward
	So true, so just, and now so comfortable?
	It almost turns my dangerous nature wild.
	Let me behold thy face. Surely, this man
	Was born of woman.

诚的同情,仍旧把他看作我的主人一样用我的生命为他服役。我的最亲爱的主人!

(泰门上前)

泰　　门　走开!你是什么人?

弗莱维斯　您忘记我了吗,大爷?

泰　　门　为什么问我这个问题?我已经忘记了所有的人了;要是你承认自己是个人,那么我当然也忘记你了。

弗莱维斯　我是您的一个可怜的忠心的仆人。

泰　　门　那么我不认识你。我从来不曾有过一个忠心的仆人在我的身边;我只是养了一大群恶汉,侍候奸徒们的肉食。

弗莱维斯　(哭泣)神明可以作证,从来不曾有过一个可怜的管家像我一样为了他的破产的主人而衷心哀痛。

泰　　门　怎么!你哭了吗?过来,那么我爱你,因为你是一个女人,不是冷酷无情的男子,男子的眼睛除了激于情欲和大笑的时候以外,是从来不会潮润的。他们的恻隐之心久已睡去了;奇怪的时代,人们流泪是为了欢笑,不是为了哭泣!

弗莱维斯　请您不要把我当作陌生人,我的好大爷,接受我的同情的吊慰;我还剩着不多几个钱在此,请您仍旧让我做您的管家吧。

泰　　门　我竟有这样一个忠心正直的管家来安慰我吗?我的狂

	Forgive my general and exceptless rashness,
	You perpetual sober gods! I do proclaim
	One honest man — mistake me not, but one,
	No more, I pray — and he's a steward.
	How fain would I have hated all mankind,
	And thou redeem'st thyself. But all save thee,
	I fell with curses.
	Methinks thou art more honest now than wise,
	For by oppressing and betraying me
	Thou mightst have sooner got another service:
	For many so arrive at second masters
	Upon their first lord's neck. But tell me true —
	For I must ever doubt, though ne'er so sure —
	Is not thy kindness subtle, covetous,
	If not a usuring kindness, and, as rich men deal gifts,
	Expecting in return twenty for one?
FLAVIUS	No, my most worthy master, in whose breast
	Doubt and suspect, alas, are placed too late.
	You should have feared false times when you did feast:
	Suspect still comes where an estate is least.
	That which I show, heaven knows, is merely love,
	Duty and zeal to your unmatchèd mind,
	Care of your food and living, and, believe it,
	My most honoured lord,
	For any benefit that points to me,
	Either in hope or present, I'd exchange
	For this one wish: that you had power and wealth
	To requite me by making rich yourself.
TIMON	Look thee, 'tis so! Thou singly honest man,

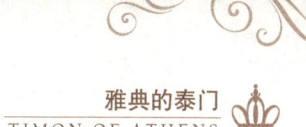

野的心都几乎被你软化了。让我瞧瞧你的脸。不错，这个人是妇人所生的。原谅我的抹杀一切的武断吧，永远清醒的神明们！我宣布这世界上还有一个正直的人，不要误会我，只有一个，而且他是个管家。但愿没有其他的人和他一样，因为我要痛恨一切的人类！你虽然不再受我的憎恨，可是除了你之外，谁都要受我的咒诅。我想你这样老实，未免太不聪明，因为要是你现在欺骗我、凌辱我，也许可以早一点得到一个新的主人；许多人都是踏在他们旧主人的颈子上，去侍候他们的新主人的。可是老实告诉我——我虽然相信你，却不能不怀疑——你的好心是不是别有用意，像那些富人们送礼一样，希望得到二十倍的利息？

弗莱维斯 不，我的最尊贵的主人，唉！您到现在才懂得怀疑，已经太迟了。当您大开盛宴的时候，您就该想到人情的虚伪；可是一个人总要到了日暮途穷，方才知道人心是不可轻信的。天知道我现在向您表示的，完全是一片赤心，我不过对您高贵无比的精神呈献我的天职和热忱，关心您的饮食起居；相信我，我的最尊贵的大爷，我愿意把一切实际上或是希望中的利益，交换这一个愿望：只要您恢复原来的财势，就是给我莫大的报酬了。

	[*Gives gold.*] Here, take: the gods out of my misery
	Has sent thee treasure. Go, live rich and happy,
	But thus conditioned: thou shalt build from men,
	Hate all, curse all, show charity to none,
	But let the famished flesh slide from the bone
	Ere thou relieve the beggar. Give to dogs
	What thou deniest to men: let prisons swallow 'em,
	Debts wither 'em to nothing, be men like blasted woods,
	And may diseases lick up their false bloods.
	And so farewell and thrive.
FLAVIUS	O! let me stay,
	And comfort you, my master.
TIMON	If thou hat'st curses,
	Stay not: fly, whilst thou art blessed and free.
	Ne'er see thou man, and let me ne'er see thee.
	[*Exit Flavius.*]
	[*Timon retires into his cave.*]

雅典的泰门
TIMON OF ATHENS

泰　　门　瞧，我已经发了财了。你这唯一的善人，（递过金子）来，拿去；天神借手于我的困苦，把财富送给你了。去，快快活活地做个财主吧；可是你要遵照我一个条件：你必须在远离人踪的地方筑屋而居；痛恨所有的人，诅咒所有的人，不要对任何人发慈悲心，听任那枵腹的饿丐形销骨立，也不要给他一些饮食；宁可把你不愿给人类的东西拿去丢给狗；让监狱把他们吞咽，让重债把他们压死；让人们像枯树一样倒毙，让疾病吸干了他们奸诈的血！去吧，愿你有福！

弗莱维斯　啊，让我留着安慰安慰您吧，我的主人。

泰　　门　要是你不愿意挨骂，那么不要停留；趁你得到我的祝福，还是一个自由之身的时候，赶快逃走吧。你再也不要看见人类的面，再也不要让我看见你。（弗莱维斯下）

（泰门退回洞穴）

Act V

SCENE I *The Woods. Before Timon's Cave.*

[*Enter Poet and Painter.*]

PAINTER   As I took note of the place, it cannot be far where he abides.

POET   What's to be thought of him? Does the rumour hold for true that he's so full of gold?

PAINTER   Certain. Alcibiades reports it: Phrynia and Timandra had gold of him. He likewise enriched poor straggling soldiers with great quantity. 'Tis said he gave unto his steward a mighty sum.

POET   Then this breaking of his has been but a try for his friends?

PAINTER   Nothing else: you shall see him a palm in Athens again, and flourish with the highest. Therefore 'tis not amiss we tender our loves to him, in this supposed distress of his: it will show honestly in us, and is very likely to load our purposes with what they travail for, if it be a just and true report that goes of his having.

POET   What have you now to present unto him?

PAINTER   Nothing at this time but my visitation: only I will promise him an excellent piece.

POET   I must serve him so too, tell him of an intent that's coming toward him.

PAINTER   Good as the best. Promising is the very air o'th'time:

第 五 幕

第一场 树林。泰门所居洞穴之前

（诗人及画师上）

画　师　照我所记得的这地方的样子，离他的住处不会怎么远了。

诗　人　他这人真有点莫测高深。人家说他拥有大量的黄金，这谣言是真的吗？

画　师　真的。艾西巴第斯就这样说，菲莉妮娅和提曼德拉都从他手里得到过金子；还有那些穷苦的流浪的兵士们，也拿了不少去。据说他给他的管家一笔很大的数目呢。

诗　人　那么他这次破产不过是有意对他的朋友们的试探罢了。

画　师　正是；您就会看见他再在雅典扬眉吐气，高居要津。所以我们应该在他伴为窘迫的时候向他献些殷勤，那可以表现出我们的热肠古道，而且要是关于他的多金的传言果然确实的话，那么我们枉道前来，也一定可以满载而归了。

诗　人　您现在有些什么东西可以呈献给他的？

画　师　我现在只是专诚拜访，东西可什么也没有；可是我将要允许他一幅绝妙的作品。

诗　人　我也必须贡献他一些什么东西；我要告诉他我准备写一篇怎样的诗送给他。

画　师　再好没有。这年头儿最通行的就是空口许诺，它会叫

it opens the eyes of expectation. Performance is ever the duller for his act, and but in the plainer and simpler kind of people the deed of saying is quite out of use. To promise is most courtly and fashionable: performance is a kind of will or testament which argues a great sickness in his judgment that makes it.

[*Enter Timon from his cave.*]

[*Unobserved by the others.*]

TIMON [*Aside.*] Excellent workman, thou canst not paint a man so bad as is thyself.

POET I am thinking what I shall say I have provided for him: it must be a personating of himself, a satire against the softness of prosperity, with a discovery of the infinite flatteries that follow youth and opulency.

TIMON [*Aside.*] Must thou needs stand for a villain in thine own work?

Wilt thou whip thine own faults in other men? Do so, I have gold for thee.

POET Nay, let's seek him:

Then do we sin against our own estate,

When we may profit meet and come too late.

PAINTER True:

When the day serves, before black-cornered night,

Find what thou want'st by flee and offered light. Come.

TIMON [*Aside.*] I'll meet you at the turn. What a god's gold,

That he is worshipped in a baser temple

Than where swine feed!

'Tis thou that rigg'st the bark and plough'st the foam,

Settlest admirèd reverence in a slave:

人睁大了眼睛盼望，要是真的实行起来，那倒没有什么稀罕了，只有那些老实愚蠢的人，才会把说过的话认真照办。诺言是最有礼貌、最合时尚的事，实行就像一种遗嘱，证明本人的理智已经害着极大的重症。

（泰门自穴中上）（未被他人注意）

泰　门　（旁白）卓越的匠人！像你自己这样一副恶人的嘴脸，是画也画不出来的。

诗　人　我正在想我应当说我预备写些什么献给他：那必须是一篇描写他自己的诗章；讽刺人世繁华的虚浮，指出那跟随在盛年与富裕后面的，是多少逢迎谄媚的丑态。

泰　门　（旁白）你一定要在你自己的作品里充当一个恶徒吗？你要在别人的身上暴露你自己的弱点吗？很好，我有金子给你哩。

诗　人　来，我们找他去吧。要是我们遇见了有利可获的机会而失之交臂，那就太对不起我们自己的幸运了。

画　师　不错，趁着白昼的光亮不用你出钱的时候，应当赶快找寻你所要的东西，等到黑夜到来，那就太晚了。来。

泰　门　（旁白）待我在转角的地方和你们相会吧。黄金真是一尊了不得的神明，即使他住在比猪窝还卑污的庙宇里，也会受人膜拜！你驾驶船只在海上航行，你使奴隶的心中发生敬羡；你是应该被人们顶礼的，让你的

	To thee be worship, and thy saints for aye
	Be crowned with plagues that thee alone obey.
	Fit I meet them. [*Comes forward.*]
POET	Hail, worthy Timon!
PAINTER	Our late noble master!
TIMON	Have I once lived to see two honest men?
POET	Sir,
	Having often of your open bounty tasted,
	Hearing you were retired, your friends fall'n off,
	Whose thankless natures — O abhorrèd spirits! —
	Not all the whips of heaven are large enough:
	What, to you,
	Whose star-like nobleness gave life and influence
	To their whole being? I am rapt and cannot cover
	The monstrous bulk of this ingratitude
	With any size of words.
TIMON	Let it go naked, men may see't the better:
	You that are honest, by being what you are,
	Make them best seen and known.
PAINTER	He and myself
	Have travelled in the great shower of your gifts,
	And sweetly felt it.
TIMON	Ay, you are honest men.
PAINTER	We are hither come to offer you our service.
TIMON	Most honest men. Why, how shall I requite you?
	Can you eat roots and drink cold water? No.
BOTH	What we can do we'll do to do you service.
TIMON	You're honest men. You've heard that I have gold,
	I am sure you have. Speak truth: you're honest men.

圣徒们永远罩着只接受你的使唤的瘟疫吧。我现在可以去见他们。（上前）

诗　　人　祝福，可尊敬的泰门！

画　　师　我们高贵的旧主人！

泰　　门　我曾经看见过两个正人君子吗？

诗　　人　先生，我常常沾沐您的慷慨的恩施，听说您已经隐居避世，您的朋友们一个个冷落了踪迹，他们那种忘恩的天性——啊，没有良心的东西！上天把所有的刑罚降在他们身上也掩蔽不了他们的罪辜！嘿！他们居然会这样对待您，他们整个的身心都在您的星辰一样的仁惠之下得到化育！我简直气疯了，想不出用怎样巨大的字眼，才可以遮盖这种薄情无义的弥天罪恶。

泰　　门　不要遮盖它，让人家可以看得清楚一些。你们都是正人君子，还是把你们的本来面目公之大众吧。

画　　师　我们两个人常常受到您的霖雨一样的赏赐，感戴您的恩泽的深厚。

泰　　门　嗯，你们都是正人君子。

画　　师　我们专诚来此，想要为您略尽微劳。

泰　　门　真是正人君子！啊，我应当怎样报答你们呢？你们也会啃树根喝冷水吗？不见得吧。

画师 / 诗人　为了替您服役的缘故，只要是我们能够做的事，我们都愿意做。

泰　　门　你们是正人君子。你们已经听见我有金子；我相信你们一定已经听见这样的消息了。老实说出来吧，你们是正人君子。

PAINTER	So it is said, my noble lord, but therefore Came not my friend nor I.
TIMON	[*To Painter.*] Good honest men. — Thou draw'st a counterfeit Best in all Athens. Thou'rt, indeed, the best: Thou counterfeit'st most lively.
PAINTER	So, so, my lord.
TIMON	E'en so, sir, as I say. [*To Poet.*] And for thy fiction, Why, thy verse swells with stuff so fine and smooth That thou art even natural in thine art. But, for all this, my honest-natured friends, I must needs say you have a little fault: Marry, 'tis not monstrous in you, neither wish I You take much pains to mend.
BOTH	Beseech your honour To make it known to us.
TIMON	You'll take it ill.
BOTH	Most thankfully, my lord.
TIMON	Will you indeed?
BOTH	Doubt it not, worthy lord.
TIMON	There's never a one of you but trusts a knave That mightily deceives you.
BOTH	Do we, my lord?
TIMON	Ay, and you hear him cog, see him dissemble, Know his gross patchery, love him, feed him, Keep in your bosom: yet remain assured That he's a made-up villain.
PAINTER	I know none such, my lord.

| 画师 | 人家是在这样说,我的高贵的大爷,可是我的朋友跟我都不是因为这缘故才来的。 |

泰门　（对画师)好一对正人君子!你画了全雅典最好的一帧脸谱,描摹得这样栩栩如生。

画师　不过如此,不过如此,大爷。

泰门　正是不过如此,先生。(对诗人)至于讲到你那些向壁虚造的故事,那么你的诗句里那种美妙婉转的辞藻,真可以说得上笔穷造化。可是虽然这么说,我的两位居心正直的朋友们,我必须说你们还有一个小小的缺点,不过这也不是什么了不得的缺点,我也不希望你们费许多的力量把它改正过来。

画师 \
诗人 ｝请您明白告诉我们吧。

泰门　你们会见怪的。

画师 \
诗人 ｝我们一定会非常感激您的开示。

泰门　真的吗?

画师 \
诗人 ｝不要疑惑,尊贵的大爷。

泰门　你们都相信着一个大大地欺骗了你们的坏人。

画师 \
诗人 ｝真的吗,大爷?

泰门　是的,你们听见他信口开河,看见他装腔作势,明明知道他不是个好东西,偏偏跟他要好,给他吃喝,把他视为心腹。

画师　我不知道有这样一个人,大爷。

POET	Nor I.
TIMON	Look you, I love you well. I'll give you gold,
	Rid me these villains from your companies:
	Hang them or stab them, drown them in a draught,
	Confound them by some course, and come to me,
	I'll give you gold enough.
BOTH	Name them, my lord, let's know them.
TIMON	You that way — and you this — but two in company:
	Each man apart, all single and alone,
	Yet an arch-villain keeps him company. [*To the Painter.*]
	If where thou art two villains shall not be,
	Come not near him. [*To the Poet.*] If thou wouldst not reside
	But where one villain is, then him abandon. [*Throws stones at them.*]
	Hence, pack! There's gold: you came for gold, ye slaves.
	You have work for me; there's payment. Hence!
	You are an alchemist, make gold of that.
	Out, rascal dogs! [*Exeunt Poet and Painter. Timon retires to his cave.*]
	[*Enter Steward and two Senators.*]
FLAVIUS	It is vain that you would speak with Timon,
	For he is set so only to himself
	That nothing but himself which looks like man
	Is friendly with him.
FIRST SENATOR	Bring us to his cave:
	It is our part and promise to th'Athenians

诗　　人	我也不知道。
泰　　门	听着,我很喜欢你们;我愿意给你们金子,只要你们替我把你们这两个坏朋友除掉:随你们吊死他们也好,刺死他们也好,把他们扔在茅坑里溺死也好,或是用无论什么方法作弄他们,然后再来见我,我一定会给你们许多金子。
画　　师 诗　　人	请您说出他们的名字来,大爷,让我们知道他们究竟是谁。
泰　　门	你向那边走,你向这边走。你们一共只有两个人,可是你们两人分开以后,各人还有一个万恶的奸徒和他在一起。(向画师)要是你不愿意有两个恶人在你的身边,那么不要走近他。(向诗人)要是你只要和一个恶人住在一处,那么不要和他来往。(向两人扔石块)去,滚开!这儿有金子哩。你们是为着金子来的,你们这两个奴才!你们替我做了工了,这是给你们的工钱;去!你有炼金的本领,去把这些泥块炼成黄金吧。滚开,恶狗!(将二人打走,返入穴内)

(弗莱维斯及二元老上)

弗莱维斯	你们要去跟泰门说话是不可能的,因为他这样耽好孤寂,除了只有外形还像一个人的他自己而外,他觉得什么都是对他不怀好意的。
元 老 甲	带我们到他的洞里去;我们已经答应雅典人,负责向

	To speak with Timon.
SECOND SENATOR	At all times alike
	Men are not still the same: 'twas time and griefs
	That framed him thus: time with his fairer hand,
	Offering the fortunes of his former days,
	The former man may make him. Bring us to him,
	And chance it as it may.
FLAVIUS	Here is his cave. —
	Peace and content be here! Lord Timon, Timon,
	Look out and speak to friends: th'Athenians
	By two of their most reverend senate greet thee.
	Speak to them, noble Timon.

[*Enter Timon out of his cave.*]

TIMON	Thou sun that comforts burn! Speak and be hanged,
	For each true word a blister, and each false
	Be as a cantherizing to the root o'th'tongue,
	Consuming it with speaking!
FIRST SENATOR	Worthy Timon —
TIMON	Of none but such as you, and you of Timon.
FIRST SENATOR	The senators of Athens greet thee, Timon.
TIMON	I thank them, and would send them back the plague
	Could I but catch it for them.
FIRST SENAROR	O, forget
	What we are sorry for ourselves in thee.
	The senators with one consent of love
	Entreat thee back to Athens, who have thought
	On special dignities which vacant lie
	For thy best use and wearing.
SECOND SENATOR	They confess

泰门说话。

元老乙　人们不是永远始终如一的；时间和悲哀使他变成这样一个人。要是命运加惠于他，恢复了他旧日的豪富，他也许仍旧会恢复原来的样子。带我们见他去，碰碰机会吧。

弗莱维斯　这就是他所住的山洞了。愿平和安宁降临在这儿！泰门大爷！泰门！出来，跟您的朋友们谈谈。雅典人派了两位最年高有德的元老来问候您了。跟他们谈谈吧，尊贵的泰门。

（泰门自穴中上）

泰　　门　抚慰众生的太阳，烧起来吧！你们有什么话？快说，说过了就给我上吊去。愿你们说了一句真话就长起一个水疱！说了一句假话就会在舌根上烂一个窟窿！

元老甲　尊贵的泰门——

泰　　门　泰门纵然落魄，也不愿见尸位素餐之辈。

元老甲　雅典的元老们问候你，泰门。

泰　　门　我谢谢他们；要是我能够替他们把瘟疫招来，我愿意把它送给他们。

元老甲　啊！忘记那些我们自己所悔恨的事吧。元老们众口一词地诚意安求你回到雅典去，他们已经考虑到许多特殊的荣典，等你回去接受。

元老乙　他们承认过去对你太冷酷无情了，现在雅典的公众已

                Toward thee forgetfulness too general gross;
                Which now the public body, which doth seldom
                Play the recanter, feeling in itself
                A lack of Timon's aid, hath sense withal
                Of it own fail, restraining aid to Timon,
                And send forth us to make their sorrowed render,
                Together with a recompense more fruitful
                Than their offence can weigh down by the dram:
                Ay, even such heaps and sums of love and wealth
                As shall to thee blot out what wrongs were theirs
                And write in thee the figures of their love,
                Ever to read them thine.

TIMON   You witch me in it,
                Surprise me to the very brink of tears;
                Lend me a fool's heart and a woman's eyes,
                And I'll beweep these comforts, worthy senators.

FIRST SENATOR   Therefore so please thee to return with us
                And of our Athens, thine and ours, to take
                The captainship, thou shalt be met with thanks,
                Allowed with absolute power and thy good name
                Live with authority: so soon we shall drive back
                Of Alcibiades th'approaches wild,
                Who, like a boar too savage, doth root up
                His country's peace.

SECOND SENATOR   And shakes his threat'ning sword
                Against the walls of Athens.

FIRST SENATOR   Therefore, Timon—

TIMON   Well, sir, I will: therefore, I will, sir: thus.
                If Alcibiades kill my countrymen,

		经感觉到他们为了不曾给泰门援手,已经失去了一座患难时可以倚靠的长城,所以他们才突破成例,叫我们前来表示歉忱,并且向你呈献他们无限的爱敬和不可计数的财富,补赎他们以往的过失。
泰	门	你们这一番话,真说得我受宠若惊,差一点要感激涕零了。借给我一颗愚人的心和一双妇人的眼睛,我就会听了这种温馨的言语而哭泣起来,尊贵的元老们。
元老甲		那么请你跟我们一同回去,在我们的雅典,也就是你的雅典,接受大将的尊位;你一定会得到人民的感谢,他们会给你绝对的权力,你的美好的声名将和威权同在。我们不久就可以逐退那来势汹汹的艾西巴第斯,他像一头横冲直撞的野猪似的,捣毁了祖国的和平。
元老乙		向雅典的城墙摇挥他咄咄逼人的剑锋。
元老甲		所以,泰门——
泰	门	好,先生,很好,那么就这样吧:要是艾西巴第斯杀

	Let Alcibiades know this of Timon:
	That Timon cares not. But if he sack fair Athens,
	And take our goodly agèd men by th'beards,
	Giving our holy virgins to the stain
	Of contumelious, beastly, mad-brained war,
	Then let him know, and tell him Timon speaks it,
	In pity of our agèd and our youth,
	I cannot choose but tell him that I care not.
	And let him take't at worst, for their knives care not
	While you have throats to answer. For myself,
	There's not a whittle in th'unruly camp
	But I do prize it at my love before
	The reverend'st throat in Athens. So I leave you
	To the protection of the prosperous gods,
	As thieves to keepers.
FLAVIUS	Stay not, all's in vain.
TIMON	Why, I was writing of my epitaph:
	It will be seen tomorrow. My long sickness
	Of health and living now begins to mend,
	And nothing brings me all things. Go, live still,
	Be Alcibiades your plague, you his,
	And last so long enough.
FIRST SENATOR	We speak in vain.
TIMON	But yet I love my county, and am not
	One that rejoices in the common wreck
	As common bruit doth put it.
FIRST SENATOR	That's well spoke.
TIMON	Commend me to my loving countrymen —
FIRST SENATOR	These words become your lips as they pass through

死了我的同胞，让艾西巴第斯知道，泰门是全不介意的。要是他把美好的雅典城劫掠一空，把我们那些善良的老人家们揪着胡须拉走，让我们那些圣洁的处女们去受那疯狂兽性的战争的污辱，那么让他知道，告诉他，泰门这样说，为了怜悯我们的老人和我们的少年，我不能不对他说，泰门对于这些是全不介意的，随他高兴怎么办就怎么办吧；因为只要你们还有不曾割断的咽喉，他们的刀是不会嫌血污的。至于我自己，那么，那横暴不法的敌人营里的每一把屠刀，都比雅典最可尊敬的咽喉更能获得我的好感。所以我现在把你们交付在幸运的天神的照顾之下，正像把一群窃贼交付给看守的人一样。

弗莱维斯　去吧，一切全都没用。

泰　　门　我刚才正在写我的墓志铭；你们明天就可以看见。健康和生活使我害了长久的病，现在我的宿疾已经开始痊愈，从虚无中间我得到了一切。去，继续活下去；愿艾西巴第斯给你们灾难，他也在你们手里遭灾，到头来大家同归于尽吧！

元老甲　我们的话都是白说。

泰　　门　可是我爱我的国家，人家虽然说我喜欢看见宗国的沦亡，其实我却不是那样的人。

元老甲　这才说得不错。

泰　　门　请你们替我向我的亲爱的同胞们致意——

元老甲　这样的话从您的嘴里出来，足见志士襟怀，毕竟与众

莎士比亚经典戏剧系列

them.

SECOND SENATOR And enter in our ears like great triumphers
In their applauding gates.

TIMON Commend me to them,
And tell them that to ease them of their griefs,
Their fears of hostile strokes, their aches, losses,
Their pangs of love, with other incident throes
That nature's fragile vessel doth sustain
In life's uncertain voyage, I will some kindness do them:
I'll teach them to prevent wild Alcibiades' wrath.

SECOND SENATOR I like this well: he will return again.

TIMON I have a tree, which grows here in my close
That mine own use invites me to cut down,
And shortly must I fell it. Tell my friends,
Tell Athens, in the sequence of degree
From high to low throughout, that whoso please
To stop affliction, let him take his haste,
Come hither ere my tree hath felt the axe,
And hang himself. I pray you do my greeting.

FLAVIUS Trouble him no further: thus you still shall find him.

TIMON Come not to me again, but say to Athens,
Timon hath made his everlasting mansion
Upon the beachèd verge of the salt flood,
Who once a day with his embossèd froth
The turbulent surge shall cover: thither come,
And let my gravestone be your oracle.
Lips, let sour words go by and language end.
What is amiss, plague and infection mend.

不同。

元老乙 它们进入我们的耳中，也像得胜荣归的勇士，在夹道欢呼声中返旆国门一样。

泰门 替我向他们致意；告诉他们，为了减轻他们的忧虑，解除他们对于敌人剑锋的恐惧，释放他们的痛苦、损失、爱情的烦恼以及在生命的无定的航程中这脆弱的凡躯所遭受的一切其他的不幸起见，我愿意给他们一些善意的贡献，指点他们避免狂暴的艾西巴第斯的愤怒的方法。

元老乙 我很高兴他说这样的话；他会重新回去的。

泰门 我有一棵树长在我的住处的附近，因为我自己需用，不久就要把它砍下来；告诉我的朋友们，告诉全雅典的人，叫他们按照各人地位的高低分别先后，凡是有谁愿意解除痛苦，就赶快到这儿来，在我那棵树未遭斧斤以前自己缢死。请你们这样替我对他们说吧。

弗莱维斯 不要再跟他絮烦了，他总是这个样子的。

泰门 不要再来见我；对雅典说，泰门已经在海边的沙滩上筑好他的万世的佳城，汹涌的波涛每天一次，向它喷吐着泡沫；到那里来吧，让我的墓碑预示着你们的命

	Graves only be men's works; and death their gain.
	Sun, hide thy beams. Timon hath done his reign. [*Exit Timon. Into his cave.*]
FIRST SENATOR	His discontents are unremovably
	Coupled to nature.
SECOND SENATOR	Our hope in him is dead: let us return,
	And strain what other means is left unto us
	In our dear peril.
FIRST SENATOR	It requires swift foot. [*Exeunt.*]

SCENE II *Before the Walls of Athens.*

[*Enter two other Senators with a Messenger.*]

THIRD SENATOR Thou hast painfully discovered. Are his files
As full as thy report?
MESSENGER I have spoke the least.
Besides, his expedition promises
Present approach.
FOURTH SENATOR We stand much hazard if they bring not Timon.
MESSENGER I met a courier, one mine ancient friend,
Whom, though in general part we were opposed,
Yet our old love had a particular force
And made us speak like friends. This man was riding
From Alcibiades to Timon's cave
With letters of entreaty which imported
His fellowship i'th'cause against your city,
In part for his sake moved.
[*Enter the other Senators from Timon.*]
THIRD SENATOR Here come our brothers.

运。让怨恨不挂唇，让言语消灭，灾难和瘟疫将会纠正一切！坟墓是人一世辛勤的成绩；隐去吧，阳光！陪着泰门安息。（下）

元老甲　他的愤懑不平之气，已经深植在天性之中，再也消解不掉了。

元老乙　我们对他的希望已经完了，还是回去凭着我们残余的力量，想些其他的办法，尽力挽救危局吧。

元老甲　事不宜迟，我们快回去。（同下）

第二场　雅典城墙之前

（二元老及一使者上）

元老丙　难为你探到了这样的消息；他的军力果然像你所说的那样雄壮吗？

使　者　他的实际的力量，比我所说的还要强大得多；而且他的行军非常迅速，大概就要到来了。

元老丁　要是他们不能劝诱泰门回来，我们的处境可真是危险万分呢。

使　者　我在路上碰见一个信差，是我旧日的朋友，虽然我们各事一方，可是我们从前的交谊使我们泯除猜忌，像朋友一般互吐真情。这个人是艾西巴第斯差他飞骑送信到泰门的洞里去的，那信上要求他协力助攻雅典，因为这次举兵一部分的原因也就是为了他。

元老丙　我们的两个同僚来了。

（甲乙元老自泰门处归）

FIRST SENATOR No talk of Timon, nothing of him expect.
　　　　　　　　The enemy's drum is heard, and fearful scouring
　　　　　　　　Doth choke the air with dust. In, and prepare:
　　　　　　　　Ours is the fall, I fear, our foes the snare. [*Exeunt.*]

SCENE III *The Woods. The Timon's Cave, and a Rude Tomb Seen.*

　　　　　　　　[*Enter a Soldier in the woods, seeking Timon.*]
SOLDIER　　[*Dislovers tomb.*] By all description this should be
　　　　　　　the place.
　　　　　　　Who's here? Speak, ho! No answer? What is this?
　　　　　　　[*Reads.*] 'Timon is dead, who hath outstretched his
　　　　　　　span.
　　　　　　　Some beast read this; here does not live a man.'
　　　　　　　Dead, sure, and this his grave. What's on this tomb
　　　　　　　I cannot read: the character I'll take with wax.
　　　　　　　Our captain hath in every figure skill,
　　　　　　　An aged interpreter, though young in days.
　　　　　　　Before proud Athens he's set down by this,
　　　　　　　Whose fall the mark of his ambition is. [*Exit.*]

SCENE IV　*Before the Walls of Athens.*

　　　　　　　　[*Trumpets sound. Enter Alcibiades with his powers
　　　　　　　　before Athens.*]
ALCIBIADES　Sound to this coward and lascivious town
　　　　　　　　Our terrible approach.

元老甲 别再提起泰门的名字,别再对他存什么希望了。敌人的鼓声已经近在耳边,一片尘沙扬蔽了天空。进去,赶快准备起来;我怕我们要陷入敌人的罗网了。(同下)

第三场 树林。泰门洞穴,相去不远
有草草砌成的坟墓一座

(一兵士上,寻找泰门)

兵 士 (发现坟墓)照他们所说的样子看来,大概就是这儿了。有人吗?喂,说话呀!没有回答!这是什么?(读墓碑)泰门死了,他的大限已到;这坟墓是什么野兽给他盖起来的,这儿是没有人住的地方。一定是死了,这便是他的坟墓。墓石上还有几行字,我可认不得;让我用蜡把它们拓下来;我们的主将什么文字都懂,他年纪虽轻,懂的事情可多哩。他现在一定已经在骄傲的雅典城前安下了营寨;攻陷那座城市是他的意志的目标。(下)

第四场 雅典城墙之前

(喇叭声;艾西巴第斯率军队上)

艾西巴第斯 吹起喇叭来,让这个怯懦的、淫秽的城市知道我们的大军已经来到。(吹谈判信号)

[*The Senators appear upon the walls.*]
Till now you have gone on and filled the time
With all licentious measure, making your wills
The scope of justice. Till now myself and such
As slept within the shadow of your power
Have wandered with our traversed arms, and breathed
Our sufferance vainly. Now the time is flush
When crouching marrow in the bearer strong
Cries of itself 'No more'. Now breathless wrong
Shall sit and pant in your great chairs of ease,
And pursy insolence shall break his wind
With fear and horrid flight.

FIRST SENATOR Noble and young,
When thy first griefs were but a mere conceit,
Ere thou hadst power or we had cause of fear,
We sent to thee to give thy rages balm,
To wipe out our ingratitude with loves
Above their quantity.

SECOND SENATOR So did we woo
Transformèd Timon to our city's love
By humble message and by promised means:
We were not all unkind, nor all deserve
The common stroke of war.

FIRST SENATOR These walls of ours
Were not erected by their hands from whom
You have received your grief, nor are they such
That these great tow'rs, trophies and schools should fall
For private faults in them.

SECOND SENATOR Nor are they living

（元老等自城墙上登城）

在今天以前，由你们胡作非为，肆行不义，把你们的私心当作公道；在今天以前，我自己以及一切睡在你们权力的阴影下面的人，谁都是叉手彷徨，有冤莫诉。现在忍无可忍的时间已经到了，蹲伏惯了的脊骨，在重重的压迫之下，喊出"受不住了"的呼声；现在无告的冤苦将要坐在你们宽大的安乐椅上喘息，短气的骄横将要狼狈奔逃了。

元老甲　尊贵的少年将军，你当初因为些微的误会一怒而去的时候，虽然你还是无拳无勇，我们无须恐惧你的报复，可是我们仍旧召你回来，好意抚慰你，用逾量的恩宠洗刷我们负心的罪戾。

元老乙　就是对于改换了形貌的泰门，我们也曾用谦恭的使节和优渥的允诺恳求他眷念我们的城市。我们并不全是冷酷无情的人，也不该不分皂白地同受战争的屠戮。

元老甲　我们这一座城墙，并不是建立于得罪你的那些人之手；这些巍峨的高塔、标柱和学校，更不应该为了私人的错误而同归毁灭。

元老乙　当初驱迫你出亡的那些人，因为自愧缺少应付非常的

                Who were the motives that you first went out:
                Shame that they wanted cunning, in excess,
                Hath broke their hearts. March, noble lord,
                Into our city with thy banners spread:
                By decimation and a tithèd death —
                If thy revenges hunger for that food
                Which nature loathes — take thou the destined tenth,
                And by the hazard of the spotted die
                Let die the spotted.

FIRST SENATOR All have not offended.
                For those that were, it is not square to take,
                On those that are, revenge: crimes like lands
                Are not inherited. Then, dear countryman,
                Bring in thy ranks, but leave without thy rage.
                Spare thy Athenian cradle and those kin
                Which in the bluster of thy wrath must fall
                With those that have offended: like a shepherd,
                Approach the fold and cull th'infected forth,
                But kill not all together.

SECOND SENATOR What thou wilt,
                Thou rather shalt enforce it with thy smile
                Than hew to't with thy sword.

FIRST SENATOR Set but thy foot
                Against our rampired gates, and they shall ope,
                So thou wilt send thy gentle heart before,
                To say thou'lt enter friendly.

SECOND SENATOR Throw thy glove,
                Or any token of thine honour else,
                That thou wilt use the wars as thy redress

才能,中心惭疚,都已忧郁逝世了。尊贵的将军,带领你的大军,高扬你的旗帜,开进我们的城中吧;要是你不顾上天好生之德,你的复仇的欲望必须得到满足,那么请你在十人中杀死一人,让那不幸接触你的锋刃的作为牺牲吧。

元老甲　不是每一个人都犯罪;因为从前的人铸下了错误而向现在的人报复,这不是合乎公道的措置;罪恶和土地一样,都不是世袭的。所以,亲爱的兄弟,带你的队伍进来吧,可是把你的愤怒留在外面。宽恕你所生长的雅典摇篮,也不要在盛怒之中把你的亲人和那些得罪你的人同时骈戮;像一个牧人一般,你可以走到羊栏里,把那些染疫的牲畜拣出,可不要漫无区别地一律杀死。

元老乙　你要什么都可以用微笑取得,何必一定要用刀剑的威力诛求呢?

元老甲　你只要一踏到我们壁垒森严的门口,它们就会砉然开启,让你仁慈的心为你先容,通报你善意的来临。

元老乙　抛下你的手套,或是任何代表你的荣誉的纪念物,表示你这次攻城的目的,只是伸雪你的不平,不是破坏我们的安全,你的全部军队可以驻扎在我们城里,直

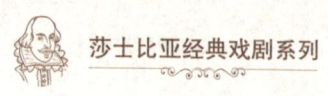

	And not as our confusion: all thy powers
	Shall make their harbour in our town till we
	Have sealed thy full desire.
ALCIBIADES	[*Throws his glove.*] Then there's my glove.
	Descend, and open your unchargèd ports:
	Those enemies of Timon's and mine own
	Whom you yourselves shall set out for reproof
	Fall and no more; and to atone your fears
	With my more noble meaning, not a man
	Shall pass his quarter or offend the stream
	Of regular justice in your city's bounds,
	But shall be remedied to your public laws
	At heaviest answer.
BOTH	'Tis most nobly spoken.
ALCIBIADES	Descend, and keep your words.
	[*Exeunt Senators, above.*]
	[*Enter a Messenger.*]
MESSENGER	My noble general, Timon is dead:
	Entombed upon the very hem o'th'sea.
	And on his gravestone this insculpture, which
	With wax I brought away, whose soft impression
	Interprets for my poor ignorance.

雅典的泰门
TIMON OF ATHENS

等我们签准了你的全部要求为止。

艾西巴第斯　（扔下手套）那么我就摔下我的手套。下来，打开你们未受攻击的城门；把泰门的和我自己的敌人交出来领死，其余一概不论。为了消释你们的疑虑、表明我的正直的胸襟起见，我还要下令严禁部下的士兵擅离营地，扰乱你们城市中的治安，凡是违反禁令的，一律交付你们按法严惩。

元老甲
元老乙　｝真是光明正大的说话。

艾西巴第斯　下来，实践你们自己的允诺。（元老等下城开门）

（一兵士上）

兵　士　启禀主将，泰门已经死了；他葬身在大海的边沿，在他的墓石上刻着这几行文字，我因为自己看不懂，已经用蜡把它们拓了下来。

ALCIBIADES   [*Reads the epitaph.*]
'Here lies a wretched corpse, of wretched soul bereft.
Seek not my name. A plague consume you wicked caitiffs left!
Here lie I, Timon, who alive all living men did hate:
Pass by and curse thy fill, but pass and stay not here thy gait.'
These well express in thee thy latter spirits.
Though thou abhorred 'st in us our human griefs,
Scornedst our brain's flow and those our droplets which
From niggard nature fall, yet rich conceit
Taught thee to make vast Neptune weep for aye
On thy low grave, on faults forgiven. Dead
Is noble Timon, of whose memory
Hereafter more. Bring me into your city,
And I will use the olive with my sword,
Make war breed peace, make peace stint war, make each
Prescribe to other as each other's leech.
Let our drums strike. [*Exeunt.*]
   [*Drums.*]

| 艾西巴第斯 | 残魂不可招,
空剩臭皮囊;
莫问其中谁:
疫吞满路狼!
生憎举世人,
殁莽海之漘;
悠悠行路者,
速去毋相溷!

这几行诗句很可以表明你后来的心绪。虽然你看不起我们人类的悲哀,蔑视我们凉薄的天性里自然流露出来的泪点,可是你的丰富的想象使你叫那苍茫的大海永远在你低贱的坟墓上哀泣。高贵的泰门死了;他的记忆将永留人间。带我到你们的城里去;我要一手执着橄榄枝,一手握着宝剑,使战争孕育和平,使和平酝酿战争,这样才可以安不忘危,巩固国家的基础。敲起我们的鼓来!(众下)

(鼓声起)